# Thom

## *Victorian Philanthropist*

A biographical essay

by Anthony Harrison-Barbet

Published in 1994 by Royal Holloway, University of London, Egham, Surrey. Design and typesetting by the Publications Unit, Royal Holloway. Printed by Castle Cary Press, 25 Brympton Way, Lynx West Trading Estate, Yeovil, Somerset.

First published in 1990 by Lyfrow Trelyspen, Gorran, St Austell, Cornwall. Revised in 1993 by Anthony Harrison-Barbet.

**British Library Cataloguing in Publication Data**
Harrison-Barbet, Anthony
    Thomas Holloway: Victorian philanthropist: a biographical essay
    1.England. Philanthropy. Holloway, Thomas
    I.Title
    361.74092

ISBN 0 900145 89 7

*For Cliona and Gavin Dando*
*(RHBNC, 1985-88),*
*with whom Thomas would have been "more than pleased".*

*100 years on - Cliona Harrison-Barbet (now Mrs Dando), gt-gt-gt-gt-niece of Thomas Holloway, being introduced to HM Queen Elizabeth, gt-gt-grand-daughter of Queen Victoria, at Royal Holloway on 16 May 1986.*

# Contents

# Preface

The life of Thomas Holloway was relatively uneventful. What is known about him concerns almost entirely his patent-medicine business and his two great benefactions - the Sanatorium and the Royal Holloway College. It is doubtful whether there is sufficient documentary material to support the preparation of a full-length biography. Nevertheless, it is surprising that so little has been written about him - no more than half a dozen or so articles in newspapers and periodicals. It is appropriate, therefore, that following on the centenary year celebrations of the College's Foundation some attempt should have been made to make up for this neglect; and I earnestly hope that this essay will go some way towards enabling not only past and present students, staff, and friends, but also the wider public to learn more about the Founder and his achievements.

Many people have kindly assisted me in the writing of the booklet. I owe a particular debt of gratitude to Miss Caroline Bingham, official historian of the Royal Holloway College, for her professional advice and expertise, and much useful information. I wish to thank also the following for their interest and for providing me with valuable details: Dr Roy Miller, Principal of the College from 1982-5; Mrs Elizabeth Bennett, the College Archivist; my relations - Mrs Beryl Catton, Rev. Darryl Chellew (Australia), Mrs Winnifred Held (USA), and Mr Michael Young; the staff of the Kingston (Surrey) and Truro Record Offices; Mr H L Douch, Curator of the County Museum, Truro; and Mr P G Laws, Lecturer in Cornish Studies, University of Exeter. Finally, and not least, I am most grateful to my wife Maeve for her encouragement and forbearance.

Anthony Harrison-Barbet, 30th June 1989

# Preface to Revised Edition

I am most grateful to Royal Holloway for taking over the publication of my biography in a much improved format. This has given me the opportunity to make a number of alterations. I wish to thank in particular Miss Anita Bates, Mrs Barbara Cotton, Mr Graham Dennis (Blacklock's Bookshop), Dr Roy Miller, Professor Alec Smith, and especially Mrs Marta Baker for co-ordinating the project.

Anthony Harrison-Barbet, April 1994

*Anthony Harrison-Barbet is a great-great-great nephew of Thomas Holloway. Educated at the Universities of Dublin, Göttingen, Oxford and Sussex, where he was awarded his doctorate in 1981, he has worked as a schoolteacher and university tutor for some twenty years, and is now a Visiting Research Fellow in Philosophy at University College, Cork. He is also the author of* **Mastering Philosophy** *(Macmillan, 1990).*

# Chapter I

# *Beginnings*

*J*n his life and achievements Thomas Holloway, the nineteenth century patent medicine manufacturer and philanthropist, epitomized the finest qualities of his age - an age of which it may be fairly said he was as much an architect as a product. Combining astute business management with a bold use of advertising on an unprecedented scale, he rapidly acquired an immense fortune enabling him to found the great institution which bears his name and which today, a century later, stands as a permanent embodiment of his vision, energy and genuine concern for his fellow men.

Thomas came of West Country stock, the first child of Thomas Holloway the elder of Plymouth Dock (now Devonport) and his wife Mary Chellew. Mary was Cornish and was born in 1776 in the village of Ludgvan, which lies due south of St Ives and some three miles north-east of Penzance. Her parents, John and Martha Chellew had been married in the same parish in 1770. Indeed, the Chellews had lived there since at least the beginning of the sixteenth century. The family name originates from a homestead built near the spring which divides the parish in two. An earlier spelling is Chylowe, from the Cornish *chy-logh*, and means the house by the water inlet. The later Chellew tenement was situated just below the spring in a small valley where the higher ground affords a magnificent view of the church and beyond to Marazion and St Michael's Mount in the Bay.

The Chellews appear to have been moderately prosperous. The parish register of 1727 mentions Henry Chilewe and John Chelewe as being among the principal inhabitants. The Rector of Ludgvan, the notable antiquarian the Reverend Dr William Borlase (1696-1772), who no doubt officiated at the marriage of John and Martha, refers in his "The Parish of Ludgvan in 1770" to a Henry Chilew as the occupier of several tenements (in Trenowys and Tremenhere) and as paying the Poor Rate, which suggests he was a man of some means. (In the same article Mary's uncle, Thomas Eva, is also listed as holding a tenement in Tregajek.) Her mother's last will, dated 1802, shows her to be the owner of three dwelling houses in Queen Street, Penzance, "lately purchased of Joseph Batten and now in the several Occupations of Thomas Rowe, Nicholas Brewer and Anthony Daw," from whom she was receiving rents. It seems therefore that Mary had been brought up - at least initially - in relatively comfortable circumstances.

The origins of Thomas's father are more obscure. It has generally been thought that the family came from Devon. But there is now some evidence to suggest that Thomas the elder was born in Portsea, Hampshire in 1766 the son of William Holloway. William had been apprenticed in 1760, though what his trade was is not known. In addition to an entry in the parish register of St Mary's, Portsea, testifying to the christening of a Thomas Holloway on 14th December 1766, there is the circumstantial evidence that two of Thomas's own children were also born in Portsmouth early in the next century, one of whom was later to marry into a Portsea family. What is certain, however, is that Thomas Holloway senior in due course joined the Royal Navy, serving in *HMS Ganges* '74 as 'Master'. (The role of a Master corresponded broadly to that of a present-day Navigating Officer; it had become a commissioned rank by the end of the eighteenth century.) He took part in the Battle of Ushant on 'The Glorious First of June' when the British Fleet under the command of Admiral Lord Howe inflicted a defeat on the French off the coast of Brittany. It would seem that Thomas retired from service soon after.

Thomas and Mary were married on 9th November 1797 at the church of Charles the Martyr in Falmouth. In the marriage entry he is

*Thomas Holloway The Elder (1766-1836) c.1824. Photograph from the Author's collection.*

described as a 'Mariner', which at that time signified the captain of any small or large vessel. Falmouth was the premier packet station in England and would have been the natural destination for any seaman engaged in the carriage of goods off the southern and south-western coasts; and even if he was not already living there it is possible that Thomas spent some time before his marriage sailing a ship of his own and plying between the Cornish port and Plymouth. Why they were married in Falmouth at all rather than in Mary's own parish is perhaps a little surprising. According to G C Boase, in his *Dictionary of National Biography* article on Thomas Holloway the younger, at the time of her marriage Miss Chellew's father was a farmer in the parish of Lelant (this is adjacent to Ludgvan). This is incorrect. Records show that John Chellew was a carpenter and that he died in 1787 in St Minver, which is some fifty miles away from Ludgvan near the north coast of Cornwall. Moreover Mary's sister Christian was baptized there in 1782. The family would therefore seem to have moved there in the early eighties. Perhaps Mary had subsequently moved south again to Falmouth to seek employment or perhaps adventure and there met her husband-to-be. Who can say?

By the turn of the century Thomas and Mary were settled in Plymouth Dock and were running a bakery in Fore Street as well as several inns in the same neighbourhood. Thomas was also able to put to good use the experience of command he had gained in the Navy, for he became a Warrant Officer in the Militia, which was then both a local police force and part of the national system of defence against the threatened invasion from France. It was in one of the inns, the Robin Hood and Little John that Thomas Holloway the younger - the subject of our essay - was born on 22nd September 1800. Given his father's several occupations, there is no reason to suppose he suffered any poverty or deprivation during his childhood. Unfortunately little is known about his early years; there is no reference to his upbringing in letters or other documents. The family do, however, seem to have been frequently on the move. While Thomas had been born in Devonport, the next two children were both born in Portsea - Mary Jane in June 1805, Henry in May 1807. A few years later Thomas senior was the landlord of an inn in Penzance. This move westwards may seem surprising, particularly as business in dockyard areas was in all probability fairly good. But it must be remembered that Mary Chellew had come from Cornwall, and even in the nineteenth century anywhere east of the River Tamar was regarded by the Cornish as 'foreign'. Perhaps she had never been reconciled to 'exile' in what were no doubt rough areas and wished to rear her family in more congenial surroundings close to her relations.

The Holloways do not appear to have moved to Penzance directly. Boase mentions that the young Thomas received his early education in Camborne. This is some twenty miles away along what is now the A30: but at the beginning of the last century roads were little more than muddy tracks and were frequently impassable. There was an omnibus service covering the 28 miles from Penzance to Truro via Camborne which, according to Boase in his *Reminiscences of Penzance*, left from the Union Hotel in Chapel Street at three in the afternoon and arrived some three hours later. Other buses and wagons, not having paid the mileage duty, were obliged to travel no faster than four miles an hour and thus took considerably longer. A daily journey to Camborne and back to visit a tutor must therefore have been out of the question. It is possible that Thomas stayed with relatives or boarded with a tutor there: but it is more likely that the Holloways actually lived in Camborne before settling in Penzance - where there were more than adequate educational facilities. The final move took place no later than 1811 when, according to W H Eva (MSS in the Royal Institution of Cornwall), "Thomas Holloway of pill fame ...... came to reside at the Turk's Head with his father". But an earlier date for their arrival cannot be ruled out. When her mother died in 1807 Mary Holloway inherited household goods and shared the rents from the Queen Street properties with her sister, and this additional income may have been instrumental in determining the Holloways to leave Portsmouth (or Camborne) shortly after.

The Turk's Head, where the family remained for at least fifteen years (and which continues little changed to this day), was the oldest inn and possibly the most ancient building in the town, dating back to the thirteenth century. Much of the house, however, had been destroyed by fire during the Spanish invasion of 1595. In the seventeenth century smugglers made use of a tunnel which connected the inn with the harbour. Further up Chapel Street was a mansion said to be haunted by the ghost of the late occupier, a Mrs Baines, who had been accidentally shot one night by a servant while she was in her orchard. Local people were thereafter fearful of entering the garden, claiming to have seen her walking around among the apple trees and even flying to sit upon the wall. Even after the ghost had been exorcized by the Reverend Singleton the house remained unlet for many years. Lower down the street St Mary's Churchyard was also believed to be the

*The Turk's Head in Penzance as it is today. Photograph from the Author's collection.*

scene of ghostly goings-on. The Turk's Head must indeed have been an exciting place for the two boys to grow up in; and we can imagine them spending many happy hours playing in and out of the narrow streets surrounding the inn and in the alley-ways at the back leading down to the harbour.

Throughout these years Thomas's education was not neglected. He may have received some grounding in Camborne, but from his arrival in Penzance the question of his schooling was taken seriously by his parents. He was assigned to Mr John Spasshat, who accepted pupils at his house in East Street. (According to Boase, Thomas also studied the violin under a Dane called Lawrance.) Spasshat was a member of a well-known Baptist family. His mother Elizabeth, who had been born in Devon, was one of nine founders of the Baptist Church in Penzance in 1802; Joseph, his father, was also a Baptist Minister there; while his brother, another Joseph, became a Wesleyan preacher.

The choice of Spasshat seems odd as the Holloways were undoubtedly Church of England. Thomas and Mary had been married in the Parish Church of Falmouth; there is a record in the subscription list of 12th April 1826 of Mr Holloway's donation of £1.00 towards the building of the new Chapel to replace St Mary's in Penzance, which was in a state of disrepair and had become too small; while in a letter written on 14th February 1872 to the Reverend T F Tyacke, Rector of St Uny, Lelant, Thomas the younger declared, "I have shut up shop altogether as regards your Church". Why, then, should the Holloways have sent their son to a member of a non-conformist family rather than entering him at the Penzance Grammar School, where Sir Humphrey Davy (by that time achieving international recognition) had been educated, and which had strong connections with St Mary's? It may be that they decided against this course because the school was in a state of transition and experiencing some difficulty in retaining its headmasters. (The Master appointed about 1812 apparently obtained the post through the submission of forged certificates and left hurriedly in 1814 when accused of having robbed a mail-coach.) Another possibility is that Spasshat was strongly recommended to them. A connection here with a certain Rev. G C Smith merits consideration.

The Rev. Smith, known to the citizens of Penzance as "Boatswain Smith", was one of the town's more colourful and eccentric characters. He was born in London in 1782 and when only fourteen was press-ganged into the Royal Navy. He became a Midshipman and then, as Master's Mate, took part in the battle of Copenhagen in 1801. After leaving the sea the following year he studied under the Reverend Isaiah Burt of Devonport from 1804-7 so as to train for the Baptist Ministry. He came to Penzance in 1807 and took over the Jordan Chapel, where he remained as Pastor until 1825. During this time he became something of a national figure. He not only founded many Baptist Chapels around Penzance but went on a mission to Wellington's army in Spain, preached in London, and started many charitable societies for seamen and their dependants. He was a prolific author of religious tracts and was frequently involved in local controversies. There must have been few citizens of Penzance in the second decade of the century who were unacquainted with this Baptist Minister and his exploits. Moreover, given his early nautical career, his sojourn in Devonport, and the fact that for many years after his arrival in the town he lived in Chapel Street, he must surely have been well-known to the Holloways. The possibility that an introduction to John Spasshat was effected by the Rev. Smith cannot therefore be discounted.

Spasshat seems to have been a successful teacher. Another of his pupils shortly after Thomas had left him, though the careers of the two boys may have overlapped for a time, was Robert Hunt, also Devonport born (in 1807). After leaving Penzance he became a doctor in London, returning briefly as a chemist and druggist in 1833-34. He was later appointed a lecturer in mechanical science at the Royal School of Mines, and in 1854 was elected Fellow of the Royal Society.

Thomas continued under Spasshat's direction until 1816. What happened thereafter is uncertain. The accepted view - no doubt following Boase's account in the *DNB* - is that his father died when the children were quite young and his widow left the Turk's Head and opened a grocery and bakery shop in Market Jew Street on the eastern side of the Old Market House adjoining the Coinage Hall. (These buildings were demolished in 1838, and Lloyds Bank now stands on the site.) The two sons, Thomas and Henry, apparently helped their mother in the shop. However, Boase's account is seriously defective in an important respect: the elder Thomas did not die in Penzance but at 4 Greyhound Place, Dun Cow Road, Bermondsey - on 13th April 1836, many years after the family had removed to London, and was buried in St James's Churchyard. Boase was of course writing some seventy years after the time of the elder Holloway's alleged demise, and his information was probably obtained from older inhabitants of Penzance or their children. Nevertheless, it is surprising that such a

*The Old Market House, Penzance 1836. Before 1830 the Holloways' grocery and bakery shop would have been in this building, probably to the right of the cart, facing down Market Jew Street. From the Author's collection.*

presumably well-known figure as the landlord of the Turk's Head should be thought to have died when there was plenty of evidence to show that he was in the town during the eighteen twenties. For example, J S Courteney in his 'Half a Century of Penzance (1825-1875)' writes: "Opposite the Wesleyan Chapel was an old inn, the Turk's Head, about 1820 and for some years after kept by Holloway, father of the famous pill manufacturer". *Pigot's Directory* of 1823 lists Thomas Holloway as a grocer (thus implying it was he who had started the business rather than his wife). A legal document attests to the assignment of a house to him on Brick Moor, Penzance in 1824. And there is of course the record of the donation of 1826 already referred to. The name does not appear in *Pigot's Directory* in 1830 however; and shortly after, on 24th August 1832, an advertisement was placed in the West Briton newspaper stating that the Turk's Head was to let: "The house is very convenient and well-situated for business in one of the principal streets of the town, attached to which there is a pump of pure water, a compact brewery, excellent beer cellars, spacious Club Room and large courtlage". The discrepancy in Boase's account is probably no more than an understandable slip, though there may be other explanations. Perhaps the rumour got about that Thomas Holloway had died at sea? It is probable that he travelled frequently. His second daughter, Caroline, was born in 1812 in Woolwich. Perhaps Mary was accompanying him while he was attending to matters relating to the running of the inn? (There is no record of either of the Holloways having relatives in the capital.) Further daughters, Matilda and Emma, were born back in Penzance in 1813 and 1821 respectively. In 1824 Thomas was in Dover; a portrait of him, now in the Royal Holloway College Gallery, seems to have been painted there. But there is no reason to suppose that Thomas did not remain with his wife and family. He left his estate to Mary, and Caroline was married in 1839 from the house in Dun Cow Road, which suggests she had been resident there for some time, certainly since her father's death in 1836.

Of more interest is what happened to the younger Thomas after he had completed his studies with John Spasshat. According to Miss Gwennol Gwaynten, writing in Volume 4 of 'Old Cornwall', he became apprenticed to Joseph Harvey, a druggist who had established a business in Market Jew Street in 1762. The article does, however, contain a number of factual errors. In addition to perpetuating the myth about Holloway senior's early death, she states that Thomas himself had been born in Penzance. It would be unwise therefore to place too much reliance on her account of his apprenticeship (records of apprenticeships in the Cornwall of that time are virtually non-existent). There was certainly a chemist's shop in Market Jew Street started by the Harvey family in 1772: but it was a William Harvey who was running the business at the time of Thomas's supposed apprenticeship, say 1816-1820, and not a Joseph. (A Mr Joseph Smith Harvey, however, was in charge during the eighteen seventies.) The possibility that young Thomas did receive some training at Harvey's chemists or druggists must not of course be ruled out. The fact that the shop was only a short way from the Holloway grocery reinforces the supposition. Moreover, he may well have been encouraged to enter such a profession by John Spasshat, whose influence is probably to be seen in the career of Robert Hunt.

Any employment Thomas may have had as a druggist's assistant could not have lasted long, for he was undoubtedly ambitious and by the eighteen twenties was probably fully aware of the limited opportunities available to him in Cornwall. There is general agreement that he left Penzance about 1828 to seek his fortune. One is tempted to speculate fancifully that he saw himself as following in the footsteps of Sir Humphrey Davy, President of the Royal Society from 1820-1827 (whose father had also come from Ludgvan): but Thomas was destined to achieve international fame in the world of commerce rather than in pure science. Whether he travelled directly to London is not known. He certainly spent some three years in Roubaix, France. Why he should have stayed in a small cloth-making town near Lille is unclear. If he had gone to London first he might have been sent abroad by an employer, or possibly he had gained an introduction through friends of his father in the capital. He also spent some time in nearby Dunkirk, where he and a few friends formed a gathering which they called the "Société de l'Étoile". One of the surviving members of this little company, a M Lambert, wrote to him in Sunninghill in 1875, and in reply Thomas said that it was in Dunkirk that he had spent some of the happiest days of his life. "Early impressions make an indelible mark on the mind, that no time or circumstance can obliterate". Whatever the reason for his sojourn in France he acquired a good grasp of the language, as entries in his letter-books show; and this was put to good use on his return to England, when, according to Boase, he took up a post as a secretary and interpreter with a firm of exporters and importers in Budge Row, EC4. This was only a mile or so from Bermondsey, where, we may assume, he was living with his parents.

# Chapter II

## *Prosperity*

By 1836 Thomas's circumstances were such as to make it possible for him to set up as a merchant and foreign correspondent on his own, initially in Wood Street, Cheapside, but thereafter at 13 Broad Street Buildings. His father's death that year was no doubt one of the factors that enabled him to embark on this venture; his mother had inherited the estate and Thomas would have been reasonably secure financially. The foundations were now being laid for his phenomenal business career.

In 1837 he was approached by a Signor Felix Albinolo from Turin. Albinolo was a leech vendor and purveyor of "Albinolo's or the St Come and St Damien Ointment", and presumably wished to consult Holloway in his capacity as merchant and agent. Holloway introduced him to Mr Travers of St Thomas's Hospital, but on discovering that the ointment differed little from the oil and wax mixtures then already in use in the hospital for the treatment of skin afflictions, the latter refused to provide Albinolo with a testimonial. However, an extract from a letter written by a Mr Joseph Green, also of St Thomas's, was included in newspaper advertisements in such a way as to suggest that he had given his approval concerning the efficacy of the product; whereupon he threatened action through the courts if the name was used again. Poor Albinolo was soon unable to meet his liabilities and on 9th October 1839 was languishing in a debtors' prison to be heard of no more.

Not long after his first meeting with Albinolo, Holloway determined to produce his own ointment in the Broad Street premises. He likewise set about obtaining testimonials and was soon in possession of one dated 19th August 1837 from Herbert Mayo, the Senior Surgeon of the Middlesex Hospital. On 15th October in the same year came the first announcement of sale of Holloway's patent preparation. Forty years later, on the anniversary eve of this first announcement, in a letter to Mr Henry Driver which Holloway directed was to be read to the staff, he recalls how the ointment had been made:

> "Tomorrow forty years ago my advertisement appeared for the first time, in three Sunday papers, the Weekly Dispatch, the Sunday Times, and another paper, the name of which I have forgotten. I have, I believe, told you that the first ointment that I made was in my mother's saucepan, which held about six quarts, an extra jump was in a long fish kettle and after that her little copper, which would hold about 40 lbs."

A further advertisement for the ointment, backed by Mayo's testimonial, appeared in the periodical *Town* on 16th June 1838. He may also have made use of Albinolo's St Thomas's testimonials, for on 4th August 1838, again in the *Town*, Albinolo wrote to warn the public that the reference in question had been given in favour of his product. Whether there had been any intention on Holloway's part to enter into a partnership, or whether Albinolo was a poor businessman, or just unlucky, can only be conjectured. Perhaps he was indeed a victim of a man with a greater determination and energy, whose sense of rectitude may have been temporarily subordinated to a more ruthless commercial will. Nor can we be certain whether it was Albinolo who had given Holloway the idea to make an ointment in the first place. If Thomas had acquired a knowledge of drugs in Penzance, as seems likely, then he may well have had it in mind for many years to manufacture a patent medicine - a cure for all ailments. But he undoubtedly possessed what Albinolo seemed to lack: initiative and perseverence, and the shrewdness to grasp from the very beginnings of his enterprise the full potential of large-scale advertising. His first

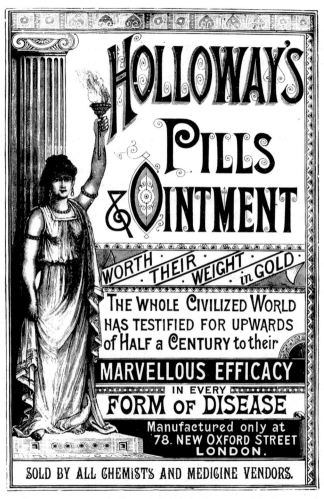

*An advertisement for Holloway's Pills which appeared in the Railway Guide, 1890. From Graham Dennis' collection.*

few years in the patent medicine business were, nevertheless, testing and the return on his advertising discouraging. As he wrote in his 'A Sketch of the Commencement and Progress of Holloway's Pills and Ointments by the Proprietor', published in January 1863:

> "My beginning was in a small way - my task very difficult and disheartening. I may add, as proof of my early discouragement, that I had expended in one week the sum of £100 in advertising, and various other ways, for the purposes of my business, and all I sold in that time was two small pots of Ointment. In fact, no person would then have accepted the Medicines as a gift. I had to practise the most rigid economy and to work most assiduously. By four o'clock in the morning I had generally commenced my day not to cease until ten at night, in order to do that myself for which I must else have paid others."

So in 1839 he started to manufacture pills in an attempt to improve profits. In the letter of 14th October 1877 he wrote:

> "Hibbert an old clerk and myself used to take turn and turn about and go into the cellar at 13 Broad Street Buildings, and make a few pills with a small machine we had, and used to put them into one of the little drawers of the desk, which was about six inches long, indeed we used to count them. This was my first beginning, and for many years ...... we used to have a little supper and singing to commemorate the event."

About this time he took to visiting the docks around Rotherhithe hoping to bring his products to the attention of the captains of ships and passengers sailing to all parts of the world - but apparently still with limited success. "My pills and ointment for a considerable time obtained little or no favour." He also resorted to subterfuge: he would arrange for his brother Henry to call in at selected shops asking for Holloway's famous pills and ointment, and to express amazement when told by the shopkeepers that they had never heard of them. Later in the day Thomas himself would enter the same stores pretending to be an agent for his own medicines and thereby secure orders.

So determined was he to succeed in selling his preparations that he soon over-reached himself in advertising: he experienced a serious cash-flow crisis and was unable to pay the many proprietors of newspapers and periodicals with whom he had entered into contracts. As a result, like Albinolo, he found himself immured for several weeks in the notorious Whitecross debtors' prison. He was released when some of his creditors, who on the strength of his previous business activities believed him to be thoroughly trustworthy, agreed to accept part payment in settlement of the sums outstanding. Several years later, to show his gratitude to those who had come to this arrangement with him, he settled up in full and gave them an extra ten per cent for their indulgence. After regaining his freedom it was not long before he was back in business and starting at last to gain some reward for his hard work and investment. Later in 1839 he moved to new premises at 244 Strand, under which address he is recorded in the *London Directory* for that year as "Mr Thomas Holloway, patent medicine Warehouse".

In 1840 he married Miss Jane Pearce Driver, then 26, the elder daughter of John Driver, a Rotherhithe shipwright. How they met or for how long he was courting her is not known: but the Drivers lived near Greyhound Place at 22 King Street and perhaps Thomas had been invited to their home having made John Driver's acquaintance while seeking to promote his medicines down by the docks. A delightful billet-doux from Thomas to Jane has been preserved, which shows something of his gallantry:

"If Grace Darling can have the permission of her Parents to go to Drury Lane Theatre this Evening she must be here by half past five o'clock.

*Portrait of Jane in 1845. From the Royal Holloway Collection.*

Grace will find that plenty of Tea and Toast well stowed away in her Lighthouse before she leaves King Street will enable her Lamp to be in good trim all the evening.

Holloway's umbrella will be as useful to him this evening as a Pot of Ointment to a bad leg."

Grace Darling was of course the daughter of the Longstone lighthouse keeper, both being acclaimed nationally for their heroism in rescuing nine people from the Forfarshire when wrecked in 1838 - probably the year in which Thomas wrote the billet-doux to Jane. The last sentence is also revealing; it betrays his commercial realism. From the start of his venture into patent medicine he was fully aware of the physiological limitations of his products: it was the convictions of his potential customers he was concerned to influence. He certainly convinced Jane of his feelings for her; they were married on 12th January 1840 at St Mary Magdalene Church, Bermondsey. He could hardly have chosen a more suitable partner; she seems to have accepted his punishing work schedule willingly and with great loyalty.

Despite the early difficulties his business started to expand rapidly and financial pressures eased as sales improved. The receipt of a small inheritance from his mother, who died on 26th March 1843 at the 244 Strand premises, also proved to be of some assistance. (In her will she cancelled his promissory notes and released him from all his debts to her. There is particular mention of £600 which "is hereby forgiven to Thomas". Had she perhaps bailed him out of the Whitecross Prison? She also left him her house in the Strand and premises in Penzance which gave him a regular income from rents.) On 6th May 1845 he opened an account at Coutts Bank with a lodgement of £409 10s.

The growing prosperity of his business is reflected in the increasing expenditure laid out on advertising. He gave the full details himself in 1877 when in order to announce his plans for his proposed College he sent a stereotyped letter to a large number of newspapers not only in the United Kingdom but also to many countries throughout the world. Whereas in 1838 he had spent £1,000 on insertions in newspapers and periodicals, and for the mentioning of his products in theatres and other places of public entertainment, by 1842 this had risen to £5,000; in 1845 he spent £10,000; £30,000 in 1855; £40,000 in 1864; £45,000 in 1882; while in 1883, the year of his death, he invested a staggering £50,000, which resulted in the return of an equal sum as clear profit. This would be equivalent to over a million pounds today. With greater expenditure he also widened the scope of his advertisements. The insertion for his ointment which appeared in the *Town* in 1838 was directed at the more leisured classes. This periodical is described by J W Dodds, in his *Age of Paradox*, in none too complimentary terms:

"Another type of publication in this half-world of London journalism was the 'Town', published by Renton 'Baron' Nicholson. It ceased publication in 1842, but was representative of a class of scurrilous salacious publications addressed to the sporting bloods. It pretended to take a high moral tone in its articles dealing with prostitution and female debasement in London. It published long, detailed accounts of prize fights (a sport illegal at the time), advertised obscene books, ran foul epigrams and poems, and gave notices of the musical and dramatic entertainments at the various saloons, particularly Nicholson's own performances at the Garrick Head, Bow Street, opposite Covent Garden Theatre."

What better periodical could there have been for the first advertisement of Holloway's all-purpose ointment! Other early advertisements included whenever possible testimonials from members of the medical profession or from the aristocracy attesting most fulsomely to the efficacy of 'Professor' Holloway's preparations. This letter dated 21st February 1845 from Lord Aldborough, then in Leghorn, is typical:

"SIR - Various circumstances prevented the possibility of my thanking you before this time for your politeness in sending me your pills as you did. I now take this opportunity of sending you an order for the amount and, at the same time, to add that your pills have effected a cure of a disorder in my Liver and Stomach, which all the most eminent of the Faculty at home, and all over the Continent, had not been able to effect; nay, not even the waters of Carlsbad and Marienbad. I wish to have another box and a pot of ointment, in case any of my family should ever require either. Your most obliged and obedient Servant."

In another standard advertisement Holloway listed some twenty of the "greatest Medical Men of their day who have either used **Holloway's** Brand **Ointment** in the Institutions to which they are attached or have recommended it in their private practices". The list contained the names of many of the Senior Surgeons of the major London hospitals, including Dr Bright of Guy's Hospital, famous for his investigations into the kidney disease named after him. This reference to Bright was, however, to lead to some controversy. The advertisement in fact mentioned two medical men of this name: "Dr Bright FRS, Ely Place, Holborn, author of several Medical works on Asthma, Dropsy, Consumption, etc.", and "R Bright MD, principal physician to Guy's Hospital". Now, in 1846 a letter appeared in *The Times* from the Lord Mayor of London claiming that Dr R Bright of Ely Place, "the celebrated physician at Guy's" had cured the ulcerous arm of a patient of some eminence as the result of applying Holloway's ointment. On 14th March the editor of The Lancet, Dr Thomas Wakley, an implacable and vehement critic of 'quackery', argued that the Dr Bright referred to (though also at Guy's) was not *the* Dr Bright (who in any case lived in Saville Row); that he was in no way "celebrated"; and that he had in fact been paid by Holloway to advertise his products! But despite a long campaign Wakley was unsuccessful in persuading the famous Dr Richard Bright to state publicly that he had at no time authorized the use of his name by Holloway for advertising

*Portrait of Thomas in 1845.*
*From the Royal Holloway Collection.*

purposes. Probably he felt the whole matter to be beneath him. To what extent Holloway lay behind the deception is unknown. But the fact that both doctors were listed in his advertisements and that the Fellowship of the Royal Society had been attributed to Bright of Ely Place instead of the Saville Row Bright, whom he refers to correctly as the principal physician at Guy's, suggests at the least that Holloway was not too concerned about accuracy. Or perhaps it was a genuine mistake?

Before long he was placing advertisements in a wider range of newspapers and periodicals, appealing to all classes in most parts of the world and in a multitude of languages, including Arabic, Chinese, Armenian, Turkish, Sanskrit, and "most of the vernaculars of India". As a result he was able to say some years later, "Among my correspondents I number Kings and Princes equally with other distinguished foreigners of all nations". Indeed, King Mongkut of Siam (of 'The King and I' fame) was so pleased with "the man who had been as it were the saviour of his country" that when an Embassy was sent to Queen Victoria Thomas was presented with an autographed letter from the King as a token of his esteem. Holloway also developed other ploys to inform the public about his medicines. He produced ballad song-sheets and published *Holloway's Almanac and Family Friend*, which contained articles about "dramatic episodes of history", blood sports and various kinds of hunting, and information about flowers. Hoardings were placed in prominent places throughout the world - not least, it is said, on the Great Pyramids themselves! It was reported in the *Tipperary Free Press* of 19th July 1877 that when a young lieutenant was asked what had struck him most on first landing in the Fiji Islands he replied, "Why, the placard posted on a pile of stones at the entrance of the harbour announcing the arrival of a hogshead of Holloway's Pills". When in 1876-77 Holloway wrote to most of the major newspapers in the world, he enclosed with his letter to each proprietor a three page circular containing a picture of himself, together with illustrations of people of various nations - including turbaned Indians sitting amidst boxes of his pills, veiled ladies from Constantinople, and pigtailed Chinamen queuing for his products.

As the demand for his medicines grew he found it necessary to extend his premises, and two houses were erected at the back of 244 Strand. This building itself was acquiring something of a reputation because of its imposing appearance; he had spared no expense to ensure that passers-by would be impressed by its ornate fittings and persuaded to purchase what was being manufactured within. However, in 1867 he had to move again to still more spacious premises at 533 New Oxford Street when the Strand building was demolished to make way for the erection of the new Royal Courts of Justice on the site. This description by a correspondent in the *Clevedon Mercury* of 23rd June 1877 gives us some idea of the uniqueness of Holloway's new headquarters:

> "The higher class officials are said to be gentlemen 'by birth and education', and accomplished linguists, so that natives of most civilized countries on calling at the office can find someone with whom they can converse. The establishment itself is most luxuriously appointed, having its dining-hall, baths, library, etc, etc. It has also a printing press, and they print and issue stereotype blocks in almost every known language. The extreme courtesy with which members of the Press, whether Metropolitan, Provincial, or Cosmopolitan, are treated form a peculiar feature in Mr Holloway's transactions. If punctuality be the soul of business, civility should be its body."

(It is also worthy of mention that he refused to pay for any advertisement unless a copy of the journal in which it was to be placed was sent to him, with the result that he accumulated at Oxford Street, as *The Times* put it after his death, "the most complete collection of English, Colonial and foreign newspapers and periodical literature in the world".)

With the expansion of his business he also soon found that he had to take on extra staff. In 1851 there were five clerks, twelve men, nine boys, and three women in the Strand premises (his Forewoman, Sarah White, was also on his household staff); by 1877 he was employing twenty-three clerks, twelve porters, and thirty-six girls; while at the time of his death there were some hundred workers in his main shop and warehouse, not counting the many travellers, agents and delivery men responsible for promoting the sales of his products. It is in the treatment of his workers that he demonstrated other qualities to which much of his success can be attributed. He was an excellent - if somewhat unconventional - employer. When first taking on a new assistant, he would pay him each night to ensure that he would return to work the next day. This came to be the established procedure, as his workmen found that being paid in this way tended to discourage them from squandering their earnings on alcohol instead of handing the money over to their wives. Indeed, Holloway always showed the greatest concern for the welfare of his employees and in this respect was perhaps ahead of his time. In the letter of 14th October 1877 to Henry Driver he writes:

"Now tomorrow I wish you to call together in my back office, all the clerks, and the porters, and to read to them the beginning of this paragraph [where he refers to the earliest days of the business], and then present to each clerk a sovereign in gold, and to the porters five shillings each in silver, and when you have done this, send for the Forewoman and all the Girls and read to them the same extract, and then give to each of the Girls, two shillings and sixpence, and to the Forewoman five shillings, and also to Mrs Knott five shillings. To the Doctor [in charge of the employees' health] read him this above, and give him a pound."

Moreover he was determined that those who had given of their best while in his employment should be rewarded when no longer able to work: that they should receive a pension - as this letter from Marion Krause shows:

> "My grandfather George Rogers was employed by Thomas Holloway for many years as a Clerk of Works (I think that was his position). I used to hear, when a little girl, how he was selected for the post, although poorly dressed in comparison with the other applicants. Mr Holloway left a directive (in his will, perhaps) that my grandfather was never to be dismissed and indeed when he could no longer go to work because of chronic sciatica, he was paid £1 a week until his death in about 1911 or 1912."

There is in fact no specific reference in any of his wills to George Rogers (who is mentioned frequently in complimentary terms in Thomas's Diary for 1877), but provision for a pension for all his long-serving employees was made in a will of 1864. Each person who shall have been in service for at least eighteen years was to receive a £20 annuity, but this would cease if the employee were convicted of felony or became bankrupt. He was also quick to reprove those in his employ who he felt had failed in their duty not only at work but, more importantly, in their own homes. He was most forthright, for example, when admonishing one of his clerks called Rough for neglecting his family. Rough's wife had complained of receiving only 6s a week, when Holloway knew that he earned 9s a day; and in his letter he remarked on the paleness of Rough's children and on the poor esteem in which he was held by the other clerks.

Holloway could be equally tough-minded when dealing with any threat to his business. In 1850 he entered into litigation against his brother Henry, who (possibly because he had been excluded for some reason from his mother's will) had started selling the pills and ointments under his own name just down the road at 210 Strand and was using labels and wrappers similar to those used by Thomas. On 9th November he obtained an injunction from the Master of the Rolls which prevented further sales by Henry. On giving his verdict the Master declared: "I think this is as clear and as plainly avowed a fraud as I ever knew, defendant will not be allowed to practice a fraud like that here complained of." Fraudulent sales abroad were less easy to deal with. In America, for example, in 1872 a certain Joseph Haydock advertised pills under the name of "Holloway & Co". Henry Driver took proceedings on Thomas's behalf but apparently without success; Haydock continued to sell his products and even resorted to skilful forgery of the wrappings to the extent of incorporating the watermark in the paper. In 1876 Holloway was forced to advertise widely in the United States to make it clear that he had no connection with Haydock. There are many instances also noted in his diaries or letters of threatened legal action against tradesmen for incorrect delivery of goods or against individuals behind with their rent on houses owned by him. At the same time he always took the greatest care to ensure his own legal expenses were cut to a minimum - as his solicitor Bowen May of Russell Square learned to his cost. "I don't intend to be out to **one farthing** of expense", Holloway wrote, "but I wish you as a **friend** to go over them [ie payments due] **very carefully** and return them to me giving your opinion con amore." On another occasion when Bowen May submitted an account for £159 16s Holloway knocked off £19 16s and then persuaded him against his better judgement to accept 35 dozen bottles of wine in lieu of cash. It seems that when in a sociable moment Holloway had once offered him a glass Bowen May remarked, "This is such a good wine, I wouldn't mind receiving this in fees." Holloway took him at his word. Bowen May tried to compromise by agreeing to accept eight dozen, but his client would not hear of it, saying that he could not possibly leave the remainder in his cellar once the batch had been broken into.

Ten years later Thomas himself was on the receiving end. On 7th November 1860 he had come to an arrangement with a Dr Sillen from Sweden who had agreed to introduce and advertise the medicines in France for the fee of £1,000. Sillen obtained a patent in Paris, but only for the ointment - "Pommade dite Holloway". Holloway therefore refused to pay. Sillen thereupon brought a successful action against him in the Court of Common Pleas. France subsequently became one country in which Thomas failed to distribute his products.

Although he delegated much of the responsibility for the sale and distribution of his pills and ointment to persons such as Dr Sillen, it was due to his own initiative and energy that agents were in the first instance sought out and appointed. As early as 1848 (and no doubt oblivious of the revolutionary turmoil into which much of Europe was falling during that fateful year) Thomas, accompanied by his wife, embarked on a "grand tour" to set up agencies and to arrange for the insertion of advertisements. They must have been remarkably energetic; although their itinerary was confined to Holland, Belgium, Germany and France, travelling by train and coach they managed to cover well over fifty towns or cities between 28th May when they left London for Antwerp and 22nd October, the date of Thomas's arrival back in the capital. (Jane returned earlier, on 1st August). A detailed account of places visited is given in his Diary: but the somewhat laconic entries are rather matter-of-fact and, apart from occasional references to the scenery, buildings of historical interest, picture galleries, and famous visitors to the various towns, are concerned largely with details of meetings with agents and general business transactions. Nevertheless he does sometimes allow himself a little more self-indulgence. Thus, in Leyden on 4th June:

"Visited the Town Hall where is the historical Picture of Van der Werff of the Siege of 1574. Saw the Catholic and Protestant Churches. 'The ruins of the Town', the University. The Museum of Natural History and that of Antiquities. Also a private Museum of a Medical gentleman who was many years in Japan. There is a famous Botanical Garden in this Town which I saw. The Fair was here a great many handsome wooden Houses with nice looking Girls at the Doors inviting people in like at some of the Houses at

A page from Thomas' travel diary of 1848. From the Author's collection.

Greenwhich Fare. Those people are from Freisland. Boorhave the Physician was born near this town."

In August he reached Germany and while in Boppard on the Rhine undertook a health 'cure' for some unspecified condition at the "cold water Establishment of Doctor Heusnen" in nearby Mühlsbad:

"Dr Herbert Mayo of Middlesex Hospital is here. Made an arrangement for 25s 4 per week and £1 for Medical attention of Dr Mayo - Arrived here at six in the Evening of Saturday. On Sunday Morning I was swaddled in Blankets for an hour and a quarter and then sprinkled all over in cold water which caused me to spring out of the Tub. I was served in this way for 3 Mornings, on the fourth I was packed in a Wet Sheet and then sprinkled with cold water but finding it did not suit my Case I gave it up. I continued at the Baths until Sunday the 3rd of Sept. when I left for Bining [ie Bingen]."

In 1851 or 1852 Holloway spent some time in America presumably to open up agencies in what promised to be a most lucrative market. No letters or diaries seem to have been written, but it is thought that his business interests in the States were later looked after by his sister Mary Jane and her husband Philip Hutchings who visited the country frequently and eventually settled there. (It would seem, however, that if any agencies were established in America, by 1876 they had been closed down - possibly as a result of the Haydock fraud. Holloway wrote to B S Barrett of New York on 7th January that year and stated, "I have no desire that my medicines should be sold in any part of the United States.") Further European travels followed. In May 1853 he embarked on an even more ambitious tour of the continent, making his way through Italy, Austria, Russia, Denmark, Germany, then back to Austria and Italy and thence by way of France home. His diary entries for this tour are unfortunately even less informative. When in Vatican City, he saw the Pope in his carriage (he was presumably unable to get close enough to sell him a box of his pills!); and later he tells us that he visited Pompeii: but apart from these occasional references and yet more names of prospective agents we learn little of his activities. He did, however, stay for some three weeks in Hamburg, where he was joined by his wife, his nephew Tom Young, and Philip Hutchings and his son Augustus.

That his journeys were entirely successful is beyond dispute if the rapid growth of his business during the eighteen fifties and sixties is any criterion. But Thomas did not rest here; he began to consider other ways by which he might add substantially to his already considerable fortune. He became a shrewd if daring speculator in stocks and shares. (His stockbroker, Sir Walpole Greenwell, was later to become one of the first Governors of the Royal Holloway College.) He kept a full account of his transactions, and in one of his Stock Books, dated January 1st 1876, he lists an extraordinarily wide range of investments made between 1858 and 1880. Trust Deeds made available after his death include the following:

£20,000 Great Indian Peninsular Railway Ordinary Stock.
£20,000 Alabama and New Orleans Texas Debentures.
£35,000 Atlantic and Great Western first leased Lines Debentures.
£20,000 Turkish Defence Loan.
£100,000 Turkish 1871 Loan.
£100,000 Mexican Government 3% 1851 Loan.
£107,750 Turkish Treasury 9% Loan.
£100,000 Peruvian 6% Loan.
5509 Alabama Great Southern B Ordinary Shares.
2000 Brazilian Submarine Telegraph Shares.

In 1880 his profit was £21,605. Such sums were almost astronomical even by nineteenth century standards; and it is understandable that Holloway was one of the few persons of his day in a position to make a loan to France in 1871 (through his own Holloway Bank) to assist that country's war effort after the Prussian invasion. Thomas also started to buy fine paintings - again as an investment rather than for any intrinsic aesthetic merit they may have possessed; we have no reason to suppose he was in any way a connoisseur. The pictures included among the effects conveyed to the Trustees of the Holloway estate on 25th August 1881 for use in the new college are nearly all by contemporary Victorian artists and are of mixed quality:

Creswick: *Trent Side* (£2,100)
Landseer: *The Bears* (£6,615)
Clarkson Stanfield: *Battle of Roveredo* (£3,465) and *Pic du Midi* (£2,677 10s)
Millais: *Princes in the Tower* (£3,990) and *Princess Elizabeth, daughter of Charles I, in Prison at St James* (£3,150)
Cooper: *Landscape and Cows* (£273) and *Landscape and Sheep* (£546)
Pyne: *Haweswater* (£273)
Copley Fielding: *Travellers in a Storm* (£3,150)
Collins: *Borrowdale* (£2,625)

Muller: *Tomb in the Water* (£2,362)
Holland: *Verona* (£913 10s)

The auctioneering of four of these works of art at Christie's (one of them being *The Bears* with its well-known legend "Man proposes, God disposes", which now dominates the Gallery and Examination Hall of the Royal Holloway College) led to much speculation in *The Times* of May 30th 1881:

> "The greatest curiosity prevailed and many questions were asked about this new purchaser in the field, and whether the name were not simply a *nom de guerre*. That this was so became the general conclusion, and it was understood that, whatever the real name of the present owner of these fine works, it is to be kept secret for the present."

In all Holloway spent £100,000 on paintings, many of which were hung in his own house before being donated to the College.

Property was another interest of his from the eighteen sixties onwards. Having appointed his brother-in-law, Henry Diggs Driver to look after the London warehouse and head office, he was able to spend some time in the country with his wife. He owned Elm House at Winkfield, a few miles south-west of Windsor. He later purchased Tittenhurst Park, in nearby Sunninghill, for £10,000 and subsequently bought forty acres of adjoining land. Then in 1869 he met a Captain Dingwall while journeying in a train to London and made him an offer for his country house, Broomfield, also near Sunninghill. The offer having been accepted with alacrity, Holloway pulled the house down, transferring a number of paintings (including Bellini's 'St Francis in Ecstasy') to Tittenhurst, and erected a new building on the site. This residence, however, he never came to occupy, and in 1872 he sold it for £20,000. Yet another estate, the Whitbourne, is mentioned in a will he drew up in 1864; and he possessed property in Cornwall (including a house he inherited from his mother), from which he received a regular rent. (There are several references in his Letter Book of 1874-1877 to Miss Pascoe of 21 Morrab Place, Penzance who sent £4 5s as the half-yearly rent for "the little house on the Green").

In 1864 Thomas and Jane took time off for a holiday - a rare event indeed. He records that they visited Matlock on 4th August and saw the house where Florence Nightingale had been born. (He was in error here; although much of her childhood was spent in Derbyshire, she was actually born in and named after the Italian city of Firenze.) On 7th October they were in Buxton, but "could not get into any of the large Hotels so came to the Shakespeare, a second rate House filled with plain people all suffering from Rheumatism". They also visited Chatsworth House; stayed at "the largest Hotel (The Granby)" in Harrowgate (sic), for 7/6 a day; went to Scarborough where they saw Frith's painting 'The Railway Station', and spent two hours in York, looking in at both the Minster and the Catholic Cathedral. (The reference to Frith's painting is of interest; commissioned for £4,500 in 1860 plus £750 for exhibition rights, it was sold in 1864 to a printseller, Henry Graves, for £16,300, from whom Holloway bought it in 1883 for a mere £2,000! It now hangs in the College Picture Gallery.)

When Thomas and his wife moved into Tittenhurst they brought with them his sister Matilda. A few years later, in 1868, they were joined by members of Jane's family: her sister Mary Ann Driver (referred to in his Diaries as "Polly"), then aged 51, and another sister Sarah ("Sally"), with her husband George Martin and daughter Celia. Her brother John Jacob Driver was a frequent visitor. A cook, housemaid, parlourmaid, and a coachman completed the entourage. This apparent takeover of the Holloway household is understandable and not at all unusual in the nineteenth century; the Drivers were all now actively involved with the running of the business, and Thomas and Jane had no children of their own.

# Chapter III

## *The Two Foundations*

As his income and possessions grew Thomas was faced with the problem of what to do with his money. Unlike many wealthy men he was not content to store up riches on earth without putting them to some use. His first intention was to make a substantial donation to his native town of Devonport. Inexplicably his offer was rejected by the Corporation. He thereupon wrote to George Godwin, a social worker and editor of *Builder*, requesting him to place an anonymous notice in his magazine to elicit ideas from readers:

> "I desire in some way or other to devote for public and useful purpose a sum equivalent to that given by the late Mr Peabody [an American philanthropist] - but I find some difficulty in discovering the best means and purposes to which such a sum could be devoted, so as to do the greatest public good, and to avoid pauperising classes who might not be eligible in public opinion for such a gift."

He also sought the advice of his solicitor; and on 13th April 1864 Bowen May accordingly wrote on Holloway's behalf to Lord Shaftesbury:

> "My Lord,
>
> A gentleman who is possessed of nearly a quarter of a million is about to make a settlement of it (after providing for his relatives) for charitable uses.
>
> Knowing your great philanthropy and your experience in such

matters, I advised him to be guided by your Lordship as to the disposal of his property, if you would condescend to take an interest in the subject. If your Lordship assents, might I ask for him the favour of an audience?

I have the honour to be,
Yr. Lordship's very obedient servant,"

Shaftesbury was of course the obvious person to consult, being perhaps the most notable social reformer of the nineteenth century. As a result of this correspondence an introduction was effected, and Holloway and Shaftesbury met at the latter's house in Grosvenor Square on 25th May. Three months later, on 1st September 1864, Holloway's first will was executed. After listing the bequests to be made to his relations and having given instructions for the continuation of the business, he directed that the residue should be "made available for charitable purposes". In particular, £150,000 was to be given to the Lord Mayor and Common Councilmen of the City of London "for the erection of a hospital for resception [sic] of convalescent patients from the London Hospitals upon such terms as my widow shall direct......to be built on lands on or about to be purchased by me". The plans were to be submitted to his wife. He went on to say that both he and his wife were to be buried in the grounds of the hospital; that a statue of himself (by Peter Hollings) was to be set up in a prominent position there; that the residue was to be invested to provide for running expenses of the business; and that pictures, statues, and pedestals were also to be bequeathed to the Lord Mayor for the hospital. Possibly on the advice of Bowen May, however, he subsequently decided that his philanthropic ambitions might be better fulfilled in his lifetime; and he wrote to Shaftesbury himself to affirm that he wished "to make generous and dignified provision for the treatment of mental illness among the less prosperous middle classes". The influence of the great reformer is apparent here; for several years earlier, in April 1861, at a meeting in the

Freemasons' Tavern (which Holloway had attended), Shaftesbury had advocated the setting-up of semi-charitable non-profit making middle-class asylums. Behind this decision lay the recognition that it was just such individuals as these whose welfare had so far been overlooked. In the Trust Deed executed in 1871 Holloway indicated that his new Sanatorium was intended for the lower middle classes, but it is clear from a report in the *Daily News* in September 1881 whom he had in mind as the eventual beneficiaries of his scheme:

> "Its purpose was to be the succour of persons of the middle class and that he had been guided by the consideration that rich people so unfortunate as to suffer from cerebral disease needed no monetary assistance, and the poor are already cared for in public asylums".

This statement was to prove significant many years later. He had intended to endow the Sanatorium with £50,000 to provide an income for its day-to-day running, but apparently later changed his mind and died before the financial question had been resolved. In 1887 £40,000 had to be found just to complete the building, and the administrators decided that persons of 'middle' and 'upper' classes would have to be admitted if the institution was to be self-supporting. Sir George Martin-Holloway - as he had then become - referred to the *Daily News* article as evidence of Holloway's true intention and suggested that the "scope of the Holloway Sanatorium includes the doctor, lawyer, clerk or any professional breadwinner whose work cannot like an ordinary business be carried on by a deputy and whose income ceases absolutely when he is unable to work".

Holloway appointed George Martin as his agent, and together they travelled widely in England and America to view other institutions. On their return a competition was held in 1871 under the Chairmanship of T C Donaldson, Professor of Architecture at University College, London, to find an architect who could be relied upon to design a building which would fully realize Holloway's own

*Holloway Sanatorium, Virginia Water.  From Graham Dennis' collection.*

45

vision. It was won from a field of twelve candidates by William Henry Crossland (with the help of John Philpott Jones), who had been a pupil of Sir George Gilbert Scott, the most prominent architect of the mid-nineteenth century. It seems from a letter to Donaldson on 18th July 1871 that Holloway had intended to take the river frontage of Somerset House (designed in the Palladian style by Sir William Chambers) as his model: but in the event Crossland's winning entry reflected the current fashion for the neo-Gothic.

In the planning of the Sanatorium (for the construction of which he donated £300,000) Holloway showed himself to be way ahead of his time. After discussions with George Martin, he decided that in contrast to the dark and depressing institutions then reserved for the poor his building should be spacious, comfortable, and welcoming; and each patient should have his own room. A recent Superintendent, Dr Roderick MacDonald, was of the opinion that Holloway

> "formulated concepts of the care and treatment of mentally ill people nearly a century ahead of current thought and which, in fact, have only become commonplace in this country in the second quarter of this century."

Certainly a remarkable amount of work went into the planning - almost the entire responsibility for which Holloway took upon himself. He spent three weeks early in 1871 visiting nearly twenty lunatic asylums in fifteen counties. And his Letter Books for 1871 and 1872 show himself fully occupied in writing to architects, doctors, directors of other asylums, builders' merchants, the Office of Works in London, and many other people from whom he hoped to obtain (free) advice about the construction and organization of his institution: the size of the rooms, the number of padded cells, number of employees and facilities for their accommodation, type of Water Closets to be installed, disposal of dirty linen, and whether tea or coffee should be considered as the more suitable for nervous and insane patients! In

1872 he was investigating schemes for cooking by gas (it saves 15% in the cost of mutton and 10% in beef, he tells us), German and Norwegian stoves, sewage processes, and the merits and prices of different kinds of bricks. To avoid delay he actually bought a brickworks himself and sold the bricks to his own builders. But, on the advice of Crossland, Portland stone was used for the dressings as bricks were proving to be too expensive. In April the first employees were engaged: a landscape gardener (for a guinea a day), a foreman (£2 a week), and a clerk of works (£2.10 a week plus 5s. for lodging). He also bought three grey mares and twenty-five handbarrows for the gardener. The first brick was laid by Mrs Holloway in May that same year.

Thomas was also responsible for laying down conditions for entry to the Sanatorium: "neither epileptic, paralytic, or presumed incurable patients can be received. Patients cannot remain for a longer period than twelve months, and no patient can be re-admitted." The institution was to be non-denominational: no one was to be excluded because of religion; and no church or chaplain was to be attached.

What of the plans outlined in his will for a convalescent hospital and, presumably, for the "incurables" who would be excluded from the Sanatorium? It seems that he was at this time determined to proceed with this second benefaction. Early in 1873 Mr Roger Eykyn, MP for Windsor and a member of the Stock Exchange received a letter from Mrs Gladstone:

"Do you think that Mr Holloway would give us the pleasure and the advantage of a little conversation with him? We have heard with **great** admiration of his **noble** schemes and a desire to do good to suffering humanity. We take a deep interest in these matters although with my husband's great engagements they must be limited as regards him. If one o'clock tomorrow happens to be a convenient hour Mr Gladstone and I would receive Mr Holloway with much pleasure or any other time might be arranged to make his acquaintance.

Perhaps I am a little vain to think I could be of any use, but I have given great attention to Convalescent & Incurable homes & I should be only thankful if I could be useful. Will you accompany Mr Holloway?

Yours sincerely,
Catherine Gladstone."

The Meeting was duly arranged and was recorded in Gladstone's diary: "June 17th, had a long conversation with Mr Holloway (of the pills) on his philanthropic plans which are very interesting."

A few days later Holloway wrote in his day-book: "Mr Eykyn came here today to communicate something to me of a private nature from Mr Gladstone." What this was is, alas, not known: but it is clear that within a few months Holloway had changed his mind about the hospital for convalescents and was beginning to formulate plans for an even more ambitious project - a college for the education of women. There were certainly precedents: in America Vassar College had been founded in 1861; while in England the College for Women opened at Hitchin in 1869 (it was renamed Girton College on being transferred to Cambridge in 1872), and Newnham College was organized in 1873 and opened two years later - though it was well on into the twentieth century before women students of the two colleges could be admitted to Cambridge University degrees. (The first university in Great Britain to extend its degrees to women was London, in 1878.) So the question of women's education was very much in the air at the time. The idea may well have been suggested to him by his wife. There is certainly no doubt about his reason for choosing to found a ladies college. This is made clear in a letter to David Chadwick, MP for Macclesfield and one of his early advisers, written some two years after he first conceived the project:

*William Henry Crossland (1835-1908). From the Egham Museum Trust.*

"Most of us who do well, are indebted in early youth to the teaching and training of our mothers - and how much better it might be to the human family if mothers of the next generation should possess a high-class education - and if anyone took a degree would not her boys and girls be formed of such a habit? and say: Mother whatever you have done in the way of learning, we will strive to emulate you."

Crossland was again appointed as architect, having suggested to Holloway that the famous Renaissance château of Chambord in the Department of Loir-et-Cher, be taken as a model for the new foundation. Crossland recalled, in an address to the Royal Institute of British Architects in 1887, the conversation which had taken place between himself and Holloway, and which had led to his being offered the assignment:

"Mr Holloway mentioned casually that he had some idea of starting another great work, and asked me whether I thought a style of architecture similar to the Sanatorium would recommend itself for the purpose. Now it appeared to me that a return either to the purer classical styles, or the Renaissance of the 16th Century was certainly impending. When, therefore, Mr Holloway invited me to submit to him illustrations of such ancient buildings as I thought suitable in style and character for the proposed College, I selected views of châteaux in the valley of the Loire, as well as that of Fontainebleau: and these I submitted, placing Chambord first. The effect on Mr Holloway was somewhat startling.

"After some complimentary remarks as to my judgement, he told me that he was advised to put the design to competition, but would like to hear from me the course I should take in the event of my becoming a competitor. I replied that I should visit the Touraine, and with an assistant sketch and measure Chambord in the completest way; also such portions of other châteaux as appeared to me useful in the study of the style and containing characteristics not found at Chambord. He then said, 'Will you do this Mr Crossland?' To which I answered most assuredly I would. He then patted me on the shoulder and said, 'My boy, you shall have the work; but mind, on the condition that you sketch and measure Chambord from bottom to top. No more competitions for me. I had too much trouble about the last'."

Crossland did indeed do as he was asked and by September he was in France with Holloway himself visiting not only Chambord but also châteaux at Blois, Amboise, Chaumont, Chenonceaux, Valeçay, Fontainebleau, and the Palace at Versailles. They were joined at Chambord by George Martin and spent several weeks measuring every room, angle, and cornice and making innumerable sketches. It was decided that the size of the rooms should be reduced from the 20'6" of Chambord to 13'6". They worked from 9.00 in the morning until 12.30 then after lunch at the Hotel back again from 2.00 until 6.30. Before leaving Holloway noted in his Diary: "I gave to one of the concierges 40 Francs to the other nothing as we considered that he did not show us that attention he should have done". They arrived home on 25th September.

Throughout the next year little more is heard of the College; Holloway seems to have been fully occupied with the Sanatorium. But from the end of 1874 he launched himself into a near frenzy of activity. He had become acquainted with a Mr James Beal, auctioneer, estate agent, and occasional journalist. On 27th October he wrote to Crossland asking him to provide Beal with details of the Sanatorium at Virginia Water and at the same time to state that "you are charged by me to build a Ladies College at Mount Lee Estate in Egham, which I have just purchased, at a cost of £25,000, and that the cost of this building will be about £150,000 ...". Crossland was to say also that the College would be larger than Wellington College and that "the founder intends that there shall be nothing like it in Europe". An article appeared in *The Times* of 29th October. On 26th November he wrote to Beal himself asking him to "act as Godfather for the two institutions, and take a prominent part as Chairman or otherwise, as you may desire, of the Board of Management...". He adds that he has seen another article in the *Building News* about the "Ladies University", for which he is greatly obliged to Beal - "The word 'University' sounds far better than College."

The next few months were spent in "sounding out" likely educationists and politicians whom he might be able to persuade to act as advisers and sit on an informal committee. Thus on 27th January 1875 he was writing to Graham Sandberg of Eton College and London Correspondent of the *Manchester Guardian*. In his letter he made it clear that the College would be secular: "The clerical influence usually so prominent will be limited to a **minimum**." He also specified elsewhere that clergymen, doctors, and lawyers should be excluded from the governing body. (Holloway placed a similar restriction on the composition of the Committee of the Sanatorium, but as Sir Lindsay Smith, a later Chairman, pointed out in his 'The Story of Thomas Holloway' in 1932, of the eight members of the House Committee elected by the General Committee two were clergymen, and all subsequent Chairmen since George Martin's death were clergymen or lawyers save one, as were most of the Deputy Chairmen. But only one medical man ever served on the Committee.) The curriculum would include modern and classical languages, algebra, geometry, physics, chemistry, botany, drawing, Mill's *Logic and Political Economy*, Green's *English History*, and "such other subjects as may be suggested by Professor Fawcett and other competent advisers". (Henry Fawcett was a significant member of Thomas's circle. Professor of political economy at Cambridge and MP for Brighton, he was also a friend and disciple of John Stuart Mill. His wife, Millicent Garrett, the sister of Elizabeth Garrett Anderson, was also to play an important part in the working out of Holloway's plans, and as the leader of the movement for women's suffrage and founder of

Newnham College was particularly well-qualified to do so.) In his letter to Sandberg Holloway goes on to say that the College would not be a training college for governesses. The Ladies' University would hold the same relation to the higher education of women as the Colleges of Oxford and Cambridge to that of men. It was typical of him to 'think big':

> "My ambition is to leave it so complete that its equal cannot be found in Europe or America......
>
> I shall take advice from all competent to give it and no effort will be spared to secure the best, and leave it as a great heritage to be carefully maintained by future generations."

In pursuance of his aims Holloway, through the good offices of James Beal, convened a private conference at his Oxford Street headquarters on 10th February 1875. He had written to David Chadwick a few days earlier about his plans, and on the same day wrote to another politician, Samuel Morley, Member of Parliament for Bristol, asking him to introduce Chadwick and various ladies who would be attending the meeting. Morley was clearly a man of some influence; a textile manufacturer and philanthropist, he was also proprietor of the *Daily News* and a member of the London School Board. The list of others present is also of significance; it included: Sir James Kay-Shuttleworth and Joshua Fitch, both educational administrators and founder members of the Girls' Public Day School Trust (Kay-Shuttleworth was particularly interested in the provision of a national system of education and teacher-training, while Fitch was an Inspector of Schools and had also been associated with the move of Girton College to Cambridge); Emily Davies, the founder of Girton, a successful agitator for the award of London University Degrees to women, and sister of the Master of The Queen's College; Millicent Fawcett; her sister, Elizabeth Garrett Anderson; Sir Edwin Ray Lankester, eminent zoologist, Fellow of Exeter College, Oxford, and recently appointed to the chair of zoology and comparative anatomy at University College, London; and the Rev. Dr William Hague, a Trustee of Vassar College, who was then visiting London.

According to the *Leeds Mercury* of 11th February, Holloway, who had never before addressed a meeting, made an interesting speech. It must also have been sufficiently effective to persuade many of his audience to give him their time and offer their advice, though it was not always accepted. He rejected, for example, the suggestion put forward by Kay-Shuttleworth that part of the new institution should be a training college and another a high school for teaching practice:

> "I desire that it shall in all respects be like a college at Oxford or Cambridge, and if there be many objections to this scheme, then I will abandon the whole thing."

And later in the year he refused to be swayed by Fawcett's argument that the exclusion of clergymen, doctors, and lawyers from the governing body could well narrow the area of selection and prejudice the future efficiency of the college.

On 20th February he wrote to Fawcett to say that he was intending to visit Oxford and Cambridge with Crossland and to request an introduction at Cambridge to gentlemen who could assist.

> "I propose that the 'Ladies University' at Egham, should be of its kind a grand imposing building that it may not by an insignificant style dishonour its name. - You are aware that nowadays, it is necessary to fill the eye."

He also sent a letter to Crossland on the same day, from which it can be seen that his vision of the college was undergoing still further expansion:

*Founder's Building, Royal Holloway. Photograph from Royal Holloway.*

"I am now just beginning to get my eyes open as to the providing of a great deal more space than was originally contemplated by us. We now propose to build a University which signifies every branch of human knowledge - .... Anatomy, Botany, Mineralogy, painting, sculpture, Law, Divinity, and I know not what else."

He asks him to bring his drawings to Oxford and Cambridge for heads of colleges, and to develop fuller plans; he knows that he (Crossland) can do anything in the way of designing and planning that is necessary.

In the event Holloway and Crossland never actually visited Oxford, but the trip to Cambridge went ahead. A full account is preserved in another letter to Fawcett. They left London on 29th March (accompanied by "a very superior man, my clerk of the works" [George Rogers], Crossland's brother, drawing boards, cartridge paper, and instruments) and stayed at The Bull, where they were "more than perfectly satisfied with the cuisine". During the next fortnight they visited every college several times, and eventually Holloway selected Trinity College "as likely to afford us the best model to work from, omitting much that appeared unsuitable for our plans". As the gateway was too large he chose for his model "a pretty little gate with belfry on the top", standing at the right of St John's. "Some interesting bits for the period were taken from other colleges."

"I am inclined to believe that the Ladies College will surpass anything of the kind at Cambridge. It will be all the one style of architecture. We cannot boast of libraries such as you have, nor Chapels, nor of some other things, but otherwise it will I think be unique of its kind."

Both Holloway and Crossland thereupon succumbed to violent colds and returned to the capital on 29th March.

What Holloway's intentions actually were at this time concerning the architectural style of the projected college are not entirely clear. In what sense was Trinity College to be taken as the model? Unfortunately, what Crossland has told us only serves to make the matter more obscure. In his 1887 address to the Royal Institute of British Architects he also referred to another conversation with Holloway which had taken place shortly before the opening of the College:

> "He never, or perhaps very seldom, praised anyone. There was, however, one exception; when, on his third visit to the College, after its completion, he once again, after six years, patted me on the back and said: 'Well done, Mr Crossland, I am more than pleased'."

The mention here of a similar incident six years previously (and therefore in 1877) must be a reference to the occasion when he was first appointed as architect for the College. But we know that Chambord was in fact measured in September 1873. So either Crossland had erroneously attributed Holloway's direction to measure the château as relating to the college rather than to the projected hospital for convalescents, or, more probably, he was wrong about the date; the offer of the new assignment having been made ten years earlier. Whichever alternative we adopt, it would seem that Crossland's memory was at fault in 1887. The most likely explanation is that Holloway did indeed decide in 1873 to build a college for women and that from the outset Chambord was selected as the model. Holloway undoubtedly thought the choice of the château (which had been the residence of French royalty until well into the eighteenth century) as most appropriate for his visionary and grandiose scheme. The stay in Cambridge must therefore be seen as enabling Holloway and Crossland to make use of buildings more accessible than Chambord so as to develop or add to their basic plans but only with respect to specific details. Trinity College, after all, although a fusion of two early fourteenth century foundations, was partly in the emerging Renaissance style of the sixteenth and seventeenth centuries. But, as Holloway said, his college was to exhibit "all the one style of architecture"; and he therefore ultimately adopted Chambord alone as providing the pattern for the College.

Thomas was now working fast. By April he had prepared a draft for the Foundation Deed, and on the 13th he wrote again to Chadwick about the place religion was to have in the College. His requirements were broadly in line with those he had set out for the Sanatorium: "I deem it necessary to declare that it shall not either now or hereafter, if my deed can prevent it, be of the religious teaching of the Church of England and, I should therefore wish that this point should be settled definitely". And he goes on to say that no church, chapel, or meeting house should be built, as he has made provision for "a very beautiful chapel where a doctrine may be preached that can offend no one". The following month he is writing to Emily Davies at Girton about the kind of examination students wishing to enter the Holloway College should take. On 4th June he is sufficiently emboldened to ask her whether "she could not be tempted hereafter to leave Girton to become the Lady Principal of the Holloway College". He inquires also whether he may ask her for advice from time to time; "there is hardly any one in the land whose experience and ability to advise me is equal to yours". Notwithstanding his flattery the Principal of Girton, presumably feeling herself to be sufficiently fulfilled at Cambridge, declined the invitation. Throughout these months George Martin was in America and was able to gather much useful information about Vassar. Holloway undoubtedly admired what was being accomplished in the American college, but he thought it too crowded with 420 students; he had suggested earlier to Fawcett that 220 should be the maximum. On 6th September he wrote to Chadwick: "I hope we shall be able to beat Vassar into fits - it shall not be my fault if we don't."

*The North Tower, Founder's Building, Royal Holloway. Photograph from Royal Holloway.*

In the midst of all this excitement and expenditure of energy the planning of the college and Thomas's personal happiness were overshadowed by the sudden death from bronchitis of his beloved wife Jane on 26th September 1875. He felt the loss keenly; she had been at his side and had been his constant support for nigh on forty years. Throughout that time there had been hardly a day when he was not at work - at head office or travelling abroad. But now for some three weeks he remained at Tittenhurst in deep mourning. He wrote no letters and received no visitors other than immediate family. (A year and a half later, on 12th January 1877, he recorded in his Diary: "This is the 37th anniversary of my marriage with poor dear Jane ...... I kissed her marble bust today in memory of her.") By the end of October, however, he had recovered sufficiently to attend to the business and to apply himself once more to matters arising out of the construction of the Sanatorium and proposals for the College which he now decided should be erected as a memorial to his wife.

Henry Driver, George Martin, and David Chadwick were appointed trustees, and on 8th May 1876 Holloway conveyed to them ninety acres of land at Mount Lee, Egham, where he intended the new institution to be built, but it was not until 14th September 1879, after plans had been completed and contracts taken up, that the first brick was laid by George Martin. In the meantime Thomas had also to attend to the building of the Sanatorium; progress was apparently slow and he was becoming impatient. When Crossland wrote to him in October 1876 asking for more money Holloway's response was characteristic. He pointed out that he had already paid Crossland £7,500 and said that there would be no more until "something happens" at the Sanatorium. Crossland had also received an advance of £500 on the College. "Let us see how the matter stands", wrote Holloway in his letter of October 4th:

"You have been preparing plans and drawings which are not and cannot be definitely settled.

Life, you know, is uncertain with us all - if anything were to happen to me my estate would be liable for engagements or debts of mine - I say nothing of what might be the result should I make advances to you - and ill-health - I will not say more, should prevent your attending to your engagement.

I do not consider that the first contract for Mt Lee will be taken until January next - before I can let you have any more money - and then the amount must not be great, I must come to a thorough understanding with you as to what footing we are to proceed upon in future with regard to advances, for something definite must be arrived at so that I may not again, as now, and for the time past, be called upon at any moment to give you a cheque in advance when nothing is fairly done.

I confess that your letter has given me considerable annoyance which for the future I must take measures to guard against ...... I wish you to believe that in writing to you in the manner I am now doing you will not consider that I esteem you less than ever."

Crossland was no doubt duly chastened by this stern admonition, and it is clear that Holloway soon came to have complete faith in his ability and initiative; for while throughout 1877 Thomas visited the Sanatorium almost daily to check out the smallest details he was at the Mount Lee site on no more than four occasions. The pictures and furniture to be used by the College were conveyed to the trustees on 5th August 1881, and on 25th he vested £300,000 of securities in George Martin and Henry Driver for its completion and endowment. One third of this was for the finishing of the buildings and furniture, and for the provision of musical instruments and a library; the remaining two thirds was to be used for the establishment of prizes and scholarships, salaries, and general running expenses. On 11th October 1883 he executed the Deed of Foundation in which he set out his Regulations, particular emphasis being laid on the kind of education he wished students to receive in the new institution:

"The curriculum of the College shall not be such as to discourage students who desire a liberal education apart from the Latin and Greek languages; and proficiency in the classics shall not entitle students to rewards of merit over others equally proficient in other branches of knowledge. The Founder believes that the education of women should not be exclusively regulated by the tradition and methods of former ages; but that it should be founded on those studies and sciences which the experience of modern times has shown to be the most valuable, and the best adapted to meet the intellectual and social requirements of the students. The Governors shall therefore be at liberty to provide instruction in any subjects or branches of knowledge which shall appear to them, from time to time, most suitable for the education of women."

Building of the College was finally completed a few weeks later and it was formally opened by Queen Victoria amidst much publicity and celebration on 30th June 1886, the new institution now being accorded the title the Royal Holloway College.

Sadly Thomas did not live to witness the opening of either the College or the Sanatorium; he died at Tittenhurst of congestion of the lungs on 26th December 1883. In his third and last will, executed on the same day as the Founder's Deed, he left his fortune and the business to his late wife's sister, Mary Ann Driver. She subsequently transferred it to Henry Driver and George Martin together with £20,000 to be used for its continuation. £50,000 was also given to George Martin's daughter Celia. Henry and George took over the management of the business and assumed the additional surname of Holloway by Deed Poll enrolled in the Court of Chancery on 20th February 1884. On 8th January they had called together all Holloway's clerks at the New Oxford Street Head Office to acquaint them with the wishes of their late employer. Each Department Head was to be given a cheque for £100 together with a further £30 a year; other employees would receive smaller sums and salary increases proportionate to the length

*Pots produced to hold Holloway's panacea ointment, post-1870.*
*Photograph from Graham Dennis' collection.*

of their service. The business remained in the control of the Driver-Holloways until 1930 when Holloway's Pills Ltd, of Chipstone Street, London W1, was taken over by Beecham's, with whose own version of patent pills the company had been competing for public favour since at least the turn of the century. But the Holloway pills survived in name at least until as recently as the nineteen fifties - ultimately, we may presume, to be transmuted into the famous powders! Holloway's Pills and Ointments although dormant is owned today by British Petroleum.

# Chapter IV

## *"Health For All"*

s a patent-medicine manufacturer Holloway was pre-eminent. The principal reasons for his remarkable success have already been alluded to: the boldness - almost brazen effrontery - of his advertising methods, his capacity for hard work, the close attention he paid to the welfare of his employees. But, above all, his customers had faith in his products. On the face of it this seems extraordinary. The range and variety of ailments for which effective treatment was claimed is breathtaking. In the 1850s the list included: ague, asthma, bilious complaints, blotches on the skin, colics, constipation of the bowels, consumption, debility, dropsy, dysentary, erysypelas, female irregularities, fevers of all kinds, fits, gout, headache, indigestion, inflammation, jaundice, liver complaints, lumbago, piles, rheumatism, retention of urine, scrofula, sore throats, stone and gravel, secondary symptoms, tic douloureux, tumours, ulcers, venereal affections, worms of all kinds, weaknesses, from whatever cause, etc. In the light of this one should perhaps be forgiven for criticizing the author of these wondrous medicaments for having failed to conquer death itself! In 1878 "Professor" Holloway, as he then styled himself (although he wisely later dropped this somewhat pretentious title), produced his own "Medical Guide for the use of missionaries and others who kindly interest themselves in recommending the use of his remedies". In his Preface he writes:

> "The prevention and cure of disease is a matter of vital importance to all mankind, possessing especial interest, however, to those who are remote from all professional aid.

To the missionary, traveller, and settler, it is of unspeakable importance to be possessed of such medical knowledge as will enable him to deal successfully with such diseases as mostly prevail, or are endemic in different climates and countries, and amongst those with whom it is his lot to dwell. It is for such alone that these few pages are compiled, in accordance with the wish of numerous friends in various parts of the world. It has been my aim in succeeding pages to offer a few such simple and practical directions for the preservation and restoration of health as will, I trust, when judiciously combined with the use of my two efficient remedies, tend to that end.

It would defeat the object of this little pamphlet to do more than call attention to a few general cases. For more ample particulars, the books of instructions surrounding each pot and box of the medicines should be referred to."

This is followed by a statement of his medical 'philosophy' - his explanation of the alleged efficacy of his patent medicines:

"Nature has furnished the human organism with a vital fluid - the Blood - on the healthy or unhealthy condition of which depends the health, nay, even life itself. In all countries, in all climates, and in every variety of the human race, this is the medium by which new material is conveyed to all parts of the body, and by which effete and waste products are removed out of it. Occasional doses of these pills even in health serve to maintain its purity, and when from any cause whatever the blood is rendered impure by accumulation or presence of noxious matter, their use should be persisted in until the 'depurating' organs (Lungs, Liver, &c.), are restored to normal action.

All diseases have one primary cause, viz., a want of purity in the blood and fluids, and, consequently, can alone be cured by their purification. The specific force of the balsamic remedy here introduced, exerts itself so that it searches out and removes complaints of every character, and in warm and unhealthy climates, by reason of this depurative action, these remedies not only cure already existing disease, but, if used in time, act as 'prophylactics', and prevent its intrusion. Here, in truth, is Health for All!!"

He then sets out precise instructions for the treatment of a wide variety of conditions. The following is typical:

### Disorders of the Liver, Stomach, and Bowels
"These are especially prevalent in tropical and other hot countries, and when the liver and stomach are affected the patient should take as many of my Pills for the first three nights as will produce two brisk motions, and then gradually decrease the dose, so as to keep the bowels only gently open. A portion of the Ointment, the size of a large nut, should be rubbed well into the surface of the body over the liver and stomach, for from twenty minutes to half an hour twice a day. During the first three or four days but little should be eaten (and that of a dry and solid kind); the patient should abstain from all beer, wines, or spirits. After the third day he may eat to the extent of his appetite, taking care that the food be of the most simple kind, eschewing broth, soups, stews, salt meat, eggs, pies, puddings, green vegetables, and fruit. Much exercise should be taken, but only when the weather is cool and dry. When the bowels are affected, causing diarrhoea or dysenteric symptoms, the doses of the Pills must be somewhat reduced, and hot flannels applied to the bowels freely before using the Ointment. In such cases the rubbing must be well attended to, and the diet restricted to articles of a farinaceous nature only, and milk. Rest (in the recumbent posture, if possible) is highly necessary also, and strict temperance."

Holloway's description of the treatment of "Sunstroke, or Insolation" is particularly amusing to the sophisticated and, dare one say, more knowledgeable twentieth century reader:

"When an attack of this kind takes place, the treatment must be prompt: the patient should at once have his head shaved and cold water applied, or even dashed on it. He should also be kept cool, and take eight of the Pills immediately, repeating the dose every twelve hours until the bowels are moved at least four or five times thoroughly, when he should be kept perfectly quiet for a few days, the bowels being gently relieved by occasional doses of the Pills. Slop diet of the most simple kind is preferable during the treatment. In hot countries, where this serious disease prevails, all who are exposed to the sun should live very temperately, and keep the bowels open by an occasional dose of the Pills."

The criticism might of course be made that by encouraging the gullible they could become exclusively reliant on his products and therefore disinclined to seek advice from the more orthodox physicians who could have been expected to effect permanent cures. Much the same point is often made today, perhaps unfairly, about alternative medicine with its emphasis on treating the whole man. Could Holloway's remedies have been harmful? This certainly seems to have been the view of Thackeray. It appears that in 1851 when attending the Great Exhibition Holloway had persuaded the journalist George Sala to introduce him to the famous novelist. Believing him to be a military man of high rank, Thackeray addressed him incorrectly but on learning that he was 'Professor' Holloway remarked, "Oh well, I made a natural mistake for you, too, must have killed your thousands". Perhaps this was a tongue-in- cheek observation. This cannot be said of the author of an article which appeared in *The Standard*, Winnipeg, on 7th July 1877, commenting on the advertising brochure Holloway had sent to the newspaper:

"The centre leaf is occupied with an engraving of Thomas himself - not at all flattering. Another leaf is devoted to a puff of the pills - showing that everywhere mankind swallows this nauseous medicated poison. And the third leaf announces that having been splendidly remunerated for circulating these drug-poisons, Mr Holloway is going to 'compound for sins he has a mind-to' by erecting the college for women ...... If his performances equal his promises, Mr Holloway will certainly do more good in spending his money than he did in making it."

Here, however, the critic is most surely wide of the mark; Holloway's pills and ointments were in reality quite innocuous - as one would realize from a consideration of their ingredients. The Druggists' *General Receipt Book* of 1850 listed the pills as containing aloes, rhubarb, saffron, and Glauber's salt; while the ointment was composed of olive oil, lard, resin, wax, and turpentine. In 1880 the *Chemist and Druggist* stated that the pills were made up of mainly aloes, rhubarb root, and ginger, together with some cinnamon, cardamom, saffron, Glauber's salt, and potassium sulphate, all held together by a "confection of roses". A British Medical Association analysis of the pills after his death showed the presence of aloes, powdered ginger, and soap. Even shortly before the business was taken over by Beecham's Ltd the formula was virtually unchanged - though the ingredients were now expressed in the customary Latin of the *British Pharmacopoeia*: *Aloe*, 36.15%; *Pulvis Zingiberis*, 42.15%; *Jalapa Pulverata*, 12.00%; *Podophyllin Resina*, 6.00%; *Sapo Purus*, 3.70%. It thus seems clear that if there was any secret accounting for the apparent efficaciousness of his preparations, it must have lain not so much in their contents as in the general commonsense advice concerning diet and life-style recommended by their manufacturer (though one might question his almost obsessive concern with movement of the bowels!).

We can appreciate why Thomas Holloway should have surpassed all other vendors of patent medicines in the nineteenth century and how he was able to accumulate such an immense fortune. But it may still seem surprising why so many people should have come to accept so readily what we today would perhaps regard as extravagant claims for his pills and ointments.  The explanation probably lies not only in his acquisition and publicizing of testimonials but in the actual wording of his advertisements - for which he himself seems to have taken direct responsibility.  A typical example is found in a popular journal, *The Grocer*, of 26th September 1863:

"Holloway's Ointments and Pills - Happiness round the Hearth. With the sore trials, temptations and accidents daily endangering health and life in large cities, it is most important to have at hand some means of stopping the budding evil, for the longer it is neglected the more wide spread is the degeneration.  Holloway's medicaments supply this great want, they are inexpensive, purchasable everywhere, can be readily used, are safe even in inexperienced hands, and perfectly reliable as healers and purifiers. Holloway's Ointment and Pills cure inflammations, abcesses and ulcerations, with a facility hitherto unknown.  Holloway's noble remedies will give relief to sufferers from skin diseases of the most revolting character, for which in bygone days a dangerous mineral was often administered with fatal consequences."

This is a clever piece of writing.  The association of his medications with the warmth of home life set against the insecurity and dangers of conurbations; the implicit contrast of the 'nobility' of his remedies with the 'revolting' character of some diseases (he was obviously referring particularly to syphilis); and his  stressing of the reliability of his preparations as against the poisonous nature of an old-fashioned 'cure' (mercury): all this shows a remarkable appreciation of the psychology of advertising, and together with his emphasis on their availability and modest cost helps us to understand the mass appeal of his pills and intment to people of all classes.  His advertisements are authoritative and inspire confidence.

It must also be appreciated that Holloway was a Victorian; and his achievements cannot be fully assessed without some consideration being given to the social and economic background of the nineteeenth century.

In 1800, the year of his birth, Britain's fortunes were at a low ebb. The thirteen American colonies had been lost in 1783; war broke out with revolutionary France two years later; and this was followed in 1797 by the naval mutinies at Spithead and the Nore. These events contributed to a major financial crisis. (Even the success at Ushant had been only partial, the French having succeeded in their primary objective in drawing the British men-o'- war away from the convoy!) But change was in the air: the foundations of the Industrial Revolution - and with it the country's greatness - had already been laid. On the international scene, Nelson's triumph at Trafalgar in 1805 would ensure Britain's maritime and commercial supremacy throughout much of the century; while land battles on the continent, culminating in the victory at Waterloo in 1815, were finally to destroy French power and would usher in a period of peace uninterrupted until the Revolutions of 1848. So by 1837, the year in which Holloway launched his ointment - and the year of Queen Victoria's accession to the throne, the country was entering upon an era of seemingly unbounded expansion. There were of course occasional setbacks. A poor harvest, for example, followed by another financial crisis, had exacerbated the sufferings of the working classes and was to lead to the resignation of Lord Melbourne, the well-intentioned but largely ineffectual Prime Minister and Queen's advisor. But much of the nation's misery at this time can be attributed, ironically, to the long process of industrialization initiated early the previous century. Technological progress and the agrarian revolution, together with growth in medical knowledge and better sanitation, had contributed to a declining death rate. This in turn resulted in a marked increase in population (from some 10 million in 1801 to 18 million in 1841) particularly in the urban centres, where conditions in the manufacturing industries were already bad; and this was to lead to much political and social unrest.

Nevertheless, the post-war years had seen the introduction of a number of reforms which would go some way towards ameliorating the lot of the poor and the evolution of a juster society. Prison conditions had been improved; associations were no longer illegal; many religious restrictions had been lifted; and there had been radical alterations to the system of parliamentary representation. Moreover, the very process of industrialization itself, whatever its evil effects in the short-term, was to bring prosperity to the nation. The development of railways and steamships, facilitated by the expansion of coal-mining and an improvement in the efficiency of factory machinery, had contributed to a trade surplus of some £40 million in the decade from 1831-41; whole inventions such as the electric telegraph, gas lighting, and the increasing use of iron and steel in the home would raise the standard of living of most wage earners by 1850. The forties was thus a period of both conflict and stability: rooted in the past, the country was yet looking to the future with confidence. Conditions could thus hardly be more propitious for far-sighted and self-reliant individuals such as Thomas Holloway, who both recognised and knew how to 'tap' the market. His slogan "Health for All" had an immediate attraction for an increasingly perceptive generation, whose expectations, as measured by improvements in sanitation, domestic comforts, and general physical and mental well-being, were rising steadily in direct proportion to their growing affluence.

From the eighteen forties onwards the expansion of Thomas's business reflected the prosperity of the country at large. Despite the occasional crises - poor harvests at home, military failure abroad - the national mood was one of buoyant optimism. The Great Exhibition of 1851 was symbolic. The population was now increasing rapidly - as were Holloway's profits. In 1851 there were some 21 million people in Great Britain; by 1881 this figure had reached nearly 30 million. Standards of health and education rose still further as a direct result of greater government involvement. A more literate and health-conscious populace naturally meant that there were more potential customers who might read advertisements and purchase his medicines. Britain, now unquestionably the "workshop of the world", controlled international trade - exporting textiles and industrial machinery, as well as the engineers and workmen who would play a major role in industrializing emergent nations in all parts of the globe. One wonders how many of these expatriates, unused to strange climates, victims of tropical diseases, gained relief from Holloway's preparations!

Finally, with economic and industrial progress came changes in the structure of society itself. The poor were of course still poor: but there were now fewer of them. Social advancement was no longer regarded as inconsistent with the preservation of rigid lines of demarcation between the several classes. Indeed, by their approbation of such virtues as hard work, thrift, and self-reliance, all of which Holloway possessed in full measure, the Victorians positively encouraged social mobility. As Thomas himself had shown, it was possible to rise from a relatively humble station in life to a position of some power and influence - in his case in the world of commerce. As he wrote in the letter of 1877, to be read to his employees:

"My object in communicating to them my early beginning is merely for their edification as showing what small beginnings may lead to, by ability, perseverance, and industry."

# Chapter V

## *Holloway - The Man*

We have described Thomas Holloway's beginnings, the growth of his business, the foundation of the two institutions, and have suggested some of the reasons for his success. But what of the man himself? The bare facts about his physical appearance are uncontroversial. He was over six feet tall and (in the eighteen fifties when on holiday) weighed some thirteen stones. As for his character, several aspects stand out and have already been alluded to. He was clearly an individual of exceptional will-power, determination, and single-mindedness, with an unshakeable faith in his own potential. How otherwise could the growth of his business have been sustained during the early years of difficulty? How otherwise could his vision of the College and Sanatorium have been translated into reality? Yet he was in many ways a very private person, and it is not easy to search out and pin down the 'inner self'. Hints are to be discovered in the several portraits made of him at various stages of his career. He was already forty-five when the earliest painting was executed (by William Scott). But from his appearance he does not seem far removed from the young man experiencing those happy days in Dunkirk with his friends of the Société de l'Étoile, when Monsieur Lambert told him "many little things about a certain D" and often made him laugh. Of his own sense of humour there can be no doubt. Yet a closer inspection of the painting shows something already of the later 'no-nonsense' Holloway, contemptuous and critical of foolishness and inefficiency, perhaps faintly sardonic. The dark-brown eyes are bright, intense and penetrating, the forehead high (this is seen more particularly in later portraits as the black curls - evidence of his Cornish ancestry - recede with advancing years) and suggestive of an intellectual depth perhaps not fully realized in his youth. A comparison of the 1845 painting with an engraving completed just before he died is also revealing; the humour is still there, but can we not also detect something of that rather melancholy disposition referred to in an article about him in the *Torquay Times* of 18th August 1877? That he had by then begun to reflect upon the value of his life and work is evident from a letter to two friends resident in Boulogne, a Mrs Morragh and a Miss M'Carthy, written two years before at a time when plans for his two institutions were at an advanced stage:

> "You say I have a gold mine. If so, it is but a very small one. Is a miner's life to be desired, always digging and plodding, and even if he does bring forth some lucre, is it really worth the cost and anxiety and time he takes to get it. You are far more to be envied than I am. You are like a couple of butterflies, disporting yourselves at your pleasure, in all climes suitable to you, with nothing to think of, but to eat, drink, and be merry. No mining to do before you eat as I have. The gold that I get I cannot eat or use about myself, so after all of what value is it to me. This I think is a piece of real philosophy."

This letter provides us with a pointer to what is perhaps the central feature of his character - its enigmatic and apparently contradictory nature. He had after all worked exceptionally hard for some forty years and was fast becoming one of the richest men in the land - though he was inclined to play this down: "As regards my business I have certainly done very well, but it is ridiculous to see what the papers say about my wealth". Yet it is clear from his analogy of the gold mine that the mere possession of money gave him no great pleasure. His diary of 1877 shows that life at Tittenhurst was simple and unostentatious, and his needs modest. Drives in the Brougham or the Sociable with his late wife's sister Mary and with George Martin, Sarah, and Celia; a few games of billiards; the occasional visit to the

Thames - these activities formed the sum total of his social life. Outside this there was only his work, the running of the business - even on Christmas Day! Boase describes him as "a plain living and abstemious man, drinking nothing stronger than claret and water". He was also a man of considerable humility - in marked contrast to the grandness of conception implicit in his philanthropic schemes and indeed in the manner by which he advertised his medicines. As he wrote to Lambert, "I don't care to talk about myself, as it looks like beating the big drum, and what one does in giving away, should rather be spoken of by others than by himself". And speak about him they did! Newspapers the world over were fulsome, indeed often hyperbolic, in their praise of his achievements. "Generous, noble-hearted Philanthropist!", wrote the *St Helena Guardian*, "he has not hoarded for his family but has presented the nation with a gift of £600,000". The *Stockport Advertiser* quoted from Shakespeare:

"It has been said that some men are born great, some achieve greatness, and others have greatness thrust upon them. A more remarkable of the second of these classes, I think, it would be difficult to find in that of Mr Thomas Holloway, whose pills and ointments are household words in every civilized age, and uncivilized country in the world. In the Wilds of Tartary, the Siberian Desert, the celestial empire, yea in the very mountains of the moon, are the praises of the great pilular deity Holloway sung, and his name blessed in every known and unknown tongue as the 'mighty healer'."

The *San Fernando Gazette* wrote:

"...if we may judge of their future results by the enormous good resulting from Holloway's world-famed Pills and Ointments, then it may be safely predicted that Professor Holloway's name will erelong rank even higher than it now does among the greatest benefactors of humanity in this or any other age."

While in the opinion of *The Standard* of Buenos Aires:

> "...could we find every successful man apply his surplus fortune in
> so philanthropic a manner, we could excuse the very pardonable
> vanity of thus immortalising himself instead of searching the
> dictionary for names such as Minerva, Jupiter, Esculapius or the
> like. Holloway is a great and good man."

Be this as it may, such eulogies as these were good for business and
could only have increased his wealth still further. There can be little
doubt that, notwithstanding his self-effacing remarks to Lambert,
Thomas fully intended that this should be so; everything he did was
planned, calculated, the results anticipated. Indeed, he admitted as
much himself; for as William Crossland wrote in the *Transactions of
the RIBA* of 1887, Holloway was "a client who sent me to school, a
man who always worked with his head, never with his heart, to use his
own words". A few of the more astute of contemporary journalists,
less prone to idealistic rhapsodizing, had of course already recognized
this. Thus, *The Standard* wrote in July 1886, a month after the
opening of the College:

> "No one owed more than he did to human credulity and ignorance.
> Like a far-seeing magician he levied a tax on the fools of his own
> time to provide a fund for the diminution of folly in the generations
> to come. It would be well if others who have traded on the
> weaknesses of their fellows would make as adequate amends."

Ten years earlier Gladstone, then in opposition, had made a speech in
County Durham in which he compared the efficacy of his own politics
to the purifying powers of the famous pills. The *Waterford Mirror*, no
doubt with a political axe to grind, thereupon linked this public
declaration with Holloway's forwarding of a cheque for £500 to Mrs
Gladstone for the relief of suffering Bulgarians: "Other pills are
swallowed in tons by the British public. ...... We suspect that Mr

*Thomas in his seventies. From the Royal Holloway Archives.*

Gladstone has been affectionately requested to try a box or two (of Holloway's) and describe the effects." The writer continues in satirical vein, "Had the ex-Premier only touched on the ointment, the cheque would certainly have been drawn for £1,000." That there had been some sort of *quid pro quo* is not beyond belief. The possibility raises the question of Holloway's own political stance. The fact that he supported the Bulgarian appeal might suggest that he favoured the Liberals and was opposed to the pro-Turkish policy of Disraeli and the Conservatives. But it is more likely that his contribution to the fund was made on strictly humanitarian grounds (and it should be remembered that at this time he had already invested in Turkish Defence Bonds). In the last analysis we have to admit that Holloway kept his views on politics to himself - if indeed he had any.

It is in his attitude to charity that we encounter what might appear to be the most glaring contradiction in Holloway's character. While ready to donate hundreds of thousands of pounds for the foundation of a Sanatorium and a College for the middle classes, he seemed often to be pusillanimous towards the poor. His private secretary had been given clear instructions to consign begging letters to the waste-paper basket. "Were he [Holloway] to respond to all of them in the manner they desire", writes the secretary to an optimistic enquirer in 1876, "he would require the coffers of the bank of England itself". This is of course eminently reasonable: but it is made clear in a letter dated 7th January 1875 to a Mrs James Bennett (of Lelant, near his mother's birthplace, and probably the widow of one of his cousins) that Holloway did in fact put aside some money for those in need:

"I [George Martin] have examined the books and find that your late husband, from first to last, what with paying the debts and gifts, had from Mr Holloway over £300. It would appear that you and your husband have always been in trouble and could never help yourselves, so long as you could get money from here, and now it appears you have other troubles and so you always will have, and from what I know of your case, I should not advise Mr Holloway to give you any further assistance, but on this occasion, having some funds in hand for charitable purposes, I send you without consulting him a Postal Order for £2 which will enable you to get the roof of your little habitation repaired."

Three months later Holloway himself had clearly lost patience; his secretary wrote again to Mrs Bennett on 17th April:

"You have been told before that from the first to last you have had over £300 from Mr Holloway and that at the time of your husband's death, your debts together with the funeral expenses were paid, your house repaired and £20 put into your hands. Mr Holloway will have nothing more to do with you. You must support yourself as other poor people have to do."

Likewise similar letters were sent in the same year to a Miss Blake of 17 Queen Street, Devonport (probably also a relation on Holloway's mother's side): "No further money can be sent; she must support herself by her own industry". And later: "Does she still live with her father? Why did he not write to Holloway himself? Why has his daughter asked for help?" At the same time he was undoubtedly generous to others. In December 1874 his secretary writes to Sister Francis, of Lismore Convent, Waterford: "I am directed by Mr Holloway to send you a post office order for 9/- and also a Box of pills together as a donation." The cynic might no doubt regard this as a sound business tactic rather than as genuine altruism. However, we have already seen how well he looked after his employees, and it is indisputable that so far as his close friends were concerned there were many occasions when in financial matters he allowed his heart rather more free play than he himself seems to have acknowledged. On 4th July 1878, for example, he wrote to the Misses Clara and Emma Ewbank of Bermondsey (presumably maids to his late wife) to advise them that in consideration of their having paid into his Coutts Bank account the sum of £300 and in accordance with their wish he undertook to grant an annuity of £30 per annum on their joint lives. "I trust", he said, "you may live for a great many years yet to come to enjoy the benefit of this small annuity." Holloway received a reply from Clara a few days later:

"I am sure you must have given the subject much careful consideration, as one always told you we relied entirely on your good judgement, knowing what a good and kind friend you have always been to us. It is a great boon to have such a judicious friend to advise with..."

It is evident that there is no real inconsistency in Holloway's attitude to the giving of money to others. "Charity", he often said, "demeans the recipient of charity". It is for this reason that he would assist only those whom he considered deserving of help - those who had worked hard all their lives but who had fallen on hard times. He had no time for idlers or loafers. His 'philosophy' of altruism had much in common with that of Samuel Smiles (whose *Self-Help* had been published in 1859). It was also all of a piece with his dislike of waste and his meticulous business habits. (Some of his accounts have been preserved, and in 1874 when he was probably earning some £40-50,000 a year he records the purchase of nibs for 6d, soft soap for 10d, and 3 pennyworth of candles!)

It is in the light of this attitude that we can make sense of the oft-repeated but unfounded allegation that his business success had alienated him from his family, and of the circumstances which led to the contesting of his will four years after his death. Before we can consider this something must be said about his relatives. Of his brother Henry little more is heard after the granting of an injunction against him in 1850, apart from occasional references in letters in the early seventies. He died in Marylebone in February 1874, and shortly afterwards Thomas mentions him in a letter to Caroline (23rd September 1875): "I think poor Henry used to go to Killicks [a boarding house in Margate]". Caroline herself was married on 11th July 1839 to David ap Thomas Young, then aged 27, the son of a London Surveyor and Merchant, the witnesses being Henry and her sister Mary Jane. At the time of his marriage David was working as a mercantile clerk, but from 1839-41 - having left his wife behind in England - he was Deputy Superintendent of the British Central American Land Company on the Mosquito Coast of Honduras and also a Magistrate there. (A fascinating account of his experiences there was published soon after his return.) In 1856 he established an engineering business in Birmingham (the Hydraulic Machine Company). He died in 1862. A brother of his, William, was the inventor of the Vesta lamp; while another relation, possibly a great-uncle, was Admiral Sir William Young, who had played an active role in helping to settle the seamen's dispute at Spithead in 1797. Caroline had clearly "married well". They had three children: David ap Thomas, Caroline Jane, later married to Dr Alfred Lee, for a time Thomas Holloway's physician, and William Henry, a nephew in whose chequered career Holloway came to take a close interest. David the younger (known as Tom) took over his late father's Birmingham business and was able to offer valuable professional advice to his uncle concerning fitments needed for the Sanatorium and College. (All the piping for the hospital came from his firm.) Thomas's sister Mary Jane was now in America; Emma married a 'gentleman' in 1841; while Matilda died at Tittenhurst in 1867 unmarried and was buried in St Michael's Churchyard, Sunninghill. Thomas and Jane had no children. Indeed, one remark in a letter to Caroline (12th June 1875) suggests he was not overfond of them - at least in his later years: "Whoever may go down to see you, must bring no children with them. I will never have any in my house as you know and you shall have none in yours. Upon this point I am most positive." He was clearly a man used to having his own way. (Though his remark may well have been an expression of his regret that he had no heir.)

In 1887 Caroline Young brought a suit to recall probate on the grounds that Thomas Holloway's will of 1883 had been drawn up as a result of undue pressure by the defendants, George Martin-Holloway, Henry Driver-Holloway, and Mary Ann Driver; and that he had not been of testamentary capacity. As has been mentioned, Thomas's first will of 1st September 1864 had contained his initial instructions for the foundation of a hospital. But he also made provision for a number of bequests. These included £300 each to his brother Henry and to Matilda; £150 each to his other sisters, Caroline Young and Mary Jane Hutchings; while £30 each was to be given to James Bennett of Copperhouse, near Camborne (presumably the Bennett to whose widow Holloway's secretary was writing in 1875), Captain George Chellew of St Ives (a cousin), Mary Ann Driver, and Clara Ewbank. At this time it was already his intention that the business should be maintained, and the executors, Charles Stretton of Sunninghill and Augustus Wakeford May, of Russell Square, London (his solicitor at that time) were given the power to effect the continuation of the firm in England for ten years. Part of the estate was to be converted into money to produce an annual sum of £2,000 for his wife. After Jane's death, he executed a second will in 1876 which directed that the business and the whole of his estate should be passed on to Mary Ann Driver. The third and final will of 11th October 1883 differed in no way from that of 1876 save that George Martin and Henry Driver were now appointed executors.

At a preliminary hearing on 11th May 1887 the plaintiff objected to the request that she should produce four anonymous letters she had claimed to possess and which purported to contain the names of witnesses who would appear on her behalf at the trial. Two of the letters were apparently addressed to her, one to her solicitor, and the fourth to her prosecuting counsel. Her objection was overruled, and nothing more seems to have been heard of these letters. At the hearing itself, before Mr Justice Butt and a special jury, Caroline claimed that the will of 11th October 1883 was in the writing of George Martin and that, while under the terms of the 1876 settlement Martin and Driver would have received nothing, they had now inherited a business worth £15-16,000 a year, and a sum of £20,000. Moreover, George Martin's daughter Celia had received £50,000 from Mary Driver. Caroline claimed further that she had been excluded from Tittenhurst since 1881, that Thomas had been completely in the hands of the Drivers, and that he had exhibited "habits" and had for fourteen or fifteen years been "peculiar". On the face of it she would seem to have made out a reasonable case.

In reply George Martin-Holloway stated that when he and his wife joined the Tittenhurst household in 1868 he entered into a loose partnership with Thomas: there was no regular arrangement, and the business in London was managed by Henry Driver. Both he and Driver had been given Alabama shares by Thomas: £10-15,000 went to Henry, while he himself received £10,000. He had also been given £50-100 for holiday trips. Martin spoke of Holloway as having a shrewd capacity at the time of the disputed will.

According to Mr Drew, surgeon and physician of Egham, Thomas was of sound mind though suffering from chronic congestion of the lungs and weakness of the heart. The defending solicitor remarked that Holloway clearly did not depend on his own pills and ointment! It was also revealed that Holloway used to allow £150 per annum to his sisters Caroline and Mary Jane. Mary Driver stated in court that she had continued these allowances after her brother-in-law's death and, moreover, had given Caroline £5,000.

After deliberation the jury found for the defendants. They did not ask for costs, and Miss Driver said she intended to continue the annual payments to the plaintiff and her sister.

The question that needs to be answered now is, if Thomas Holloway was not in some sense "in the hands of the Drivers" after his wife's death, why did he make Mary Driver the sole legatee, thereby seemingly denying his own sister any access to his enormous fortune? Henry Driver and George Martin had of course shown themselves to be valuable in the running of the business; while Mary Driver had no doubt proved herself to be a reliable and caring companion for his wife. That Holloway would wish to reward them is therefore not surprising. But what of Caroline? Although she too had married a 'gentleman' who presumably had received an adequate income from his several occupations, he had died when only fifty; and it is unlikely that Caroline's circumstances were anything other than modest. There is some evidence in addition to what was revealed by Mary Driver's testimony to show that Holloway had concerned himself greatly with her welfare and that of her children. For example, we have his copy of a letter dated 12th June 1875 to Caroline, then living in Canonbury, North London:

"I have your letter from the country by which I learn you would be home this evening and that you intend going to Margate this day week and that you desire to stay there a couple of months. Pray do so by all means and at my charge. I presume you intend to invite different members down to see you for a week or so. I am glad to think that by so doing you will be able to afford pleasure to others who may come to see you and at the same time making your sojourn there in every way most agreeable. I can only say that I wish you to do the thing well, very well, .....

I send you enclosed a cheque for £50 which you must endorse and Willie will get you the money - £25 will be for your quarter up to the 1st next month £3 on account of Willie's rent and then there will be £22 towards your expenses at Margate - you will want a great deal more I know, but all you require you shall have. I don't want any accounts kept. If you send any I'll not look at them. Before you leave I will send Richard to you for the little things Jane sent up. I am here today, as you will understand. If you did not wish to keep Clara [?Ewbank] more than 4 weeks which I think will be a good long holyday for her and then to have somebody else down in her place you can do so. I don't see any objection to this. ...."

In view of the undoubted generosity shown by this letter one wonders why Holloway did not make over to Caroline a substantial sum in his 1876 will - only a year later. The explanation almost certainly lies with the character of his nephew William Henry Young - her younger son. Thomas had always taken a considerable interest in his career. An early desire of William's was to study law so as to become a solicitor; and Holloway had provided him with financial support to enable him to realize his ambition. But it seems that he failed to complete his studies. (Family tradition has it that William was nevertheless not averse to making use of his knowledge of the law to engage in occasional dubious business practices!) Through his uncle's good offices he subsequently took up a clerical position in a bank. Thomas wrote a reference for him to a Mr Tattershall in January 1872:

"In reply to your letter of the 27th instant received here this morning I beg to say that I see very little of Mr Young; but from what I have heard, I believe him to be a very industrious fellow, and indeed I have no reason to doubt his honesty so that on learning he was likely to obtain a situation as clerk at the Alliance Bank I wrote to Mr Greenwell my stockbroker to acquaint the Manager that I would, if necessary, become a Guarantee for Mr Young in any amount that may be deemed necessary."

Within a few years, however, there seems to have been a question mark about William's health, though his frequent absences from work may also suggest that he was now finding his occupation not altogether congenial (and this at a time when he was ten years married and the father of five children). Thomas wrote again to Caroline on 23rd September 1875:

"I now write in haste to say that I have a letter from Willie this morning, who it appears is off duty.

Now I would advise him not to make it appear at the bank that his health is delicate, or that his chest is permanently weak or they will assuredly take the first opportunity of getting rid of a young hand who has an indifferent constitution.

If he wishes to be put into another department, let him ask this as a temporary measure, and if he is removed, no doubt he will remain. Now if Alfred [Dr Lee] thought that a certificate of his would get him a fortnight's leave or more, and he choose to go to Margate for the time and to a good Boarding House where he will have good feeding and society, I will bear all the expense. ..."

Holloway thereupon wrote to Dr Lee on 25th September asking him to "manufacture" another certificate so that Willie could recuperate. (If his health was indeed delicate, then this trip to Margate must have worked wonders; he lived for a further forty-five years, married twice more, and died in 1920 at the age of seventy-five!)

William did in due course leave the bank: more probably he was dismissed. It is clear that about this time Holloway was becoming impatient with his nephew. The tone in a letter of 8th May 1878 is more peremptory:

"My dear Willie,

You state that the majority of your Mother's furniture is sold and you wish the exception of a few things which are left behind for your use and that your mother leaves Albert Road next week [she had moved to Albert Road, Hornsey in September 1876].

Why you send me your Railway Ticket I know not. I can give you no advice how to act. I do not presume that it is your intention to

occupy Albert Road - if you have the means to do so well and
good: but if your Mother has left you will of course do the same.

Now as regards your holidays this must be a matter that concerns
you - it does not me.
Yours ever".

It would seem from this reference to William's intentions that he was
no longer with his wife and children. This was certainly the case a
year later. Having left the bank and his family he proceeded to eke out
a precarious existence as an actor; and on 26th May 1879 George
Martin wrote to William's wife Georgiana (then only 31) at
Holloway's request:

"Your two letters have been received by your uncle. As he told you
in his last he should not write to you again. I am doing so to let you
know his resolve concerning you.

Your husband has gone away. He must be brought back and must
support you. If you or some friend were to write to Miss
Swanborough at the Strand Theatre acquainting her that your
husband has gone away and left you perfectly destitute and had
only sent you 10/- since he left and beg of her to have him
dismissed that he may return home, it would bring him back.

It is of no use for him to talk about not being desirous to shew
himself in London - he has reduced himself to a position scarcely
above that of a labourer and which you and he must realize. We all
pity **you** from our hearts but your uncle will give you no more
money - not one shilling however great your distress may be -
should you ever have to go into the Union. Do not then for a
moment fancy that your prayers - or your distress - will have any
effect upon him - so take your measures accordingly.

I desire that you understand that your uncle would have been most willing to have assisted you and your children - had your wretched and most worthless Husband instead of leaving you had sought employment of some kind or other but to go away believing that his uncle would support you he will find, to your sorrow, that he will do nothing of the kind.

When your uncle heard on February 7 last of the trouble that had come upon you he immediately came to your relief and he would have continued to assist you - but when he found out that it was expected that your Husband, while vagabondizing about the country, should rely upon your uncle to support you and your Family for evermore it became necessary he considered to **withold** from you the smallest kind of relief so that your Husband should be compelled to return to support you.

I will say no more of this distressing business. It does not appear to me or any of the Family here that you would have sufficient strength to leave your House earlier than a fortnight from this time when B... [?] would not I am sure cancel the lease. It is fortunate for you as you may now remain in it without rent until the 29 September, your uncle paying the rent and taxes. This in your deep distress may be of some little consolation to you.

Alfred Lee has written to your uncle since seeing you on Sunday and believes you to be in great distress.

It is decided that no reply shall be made to his letter after what you have said so as not to compromise you in his good opinion.

If at any time you shall write again just tell me as near as you can exactly the amount of money - or groceries -that Jenny has given you. It shall not be mentioned to them again.

I cannot conclude without assuring you that although I find it necessary to write this very sad epistle to you - your uncle wishes you to understand that you have in no way forfeited his good opinion of you - but in saying this - do not deceive yourself in thinking he will ever send you any more money - your Husband must come back and support you."

This is the stuff of which Victorian melodrama is made and it perhaps shows Holloway at his most uncompromising. Of course, to many of us in these days of a welfare state his refusal to come to the assistance of his nephew's family may seem to be unduly harsh: but it has to be recognized that his decision was entirely consistent with his principles. Moreover, Holloway's stand had the desired effect; William soon returned to his wife and children, and opened up as a pork butcher in Finsbury Park! He seems also to have continued to find an outlet for his acting potential: during the eighties he appeared with his daughter Georgiana in minor roles on the stage of the Royal Court Theatre.

In matters of business, in his lack of financial acumen, and in his general unreliability William was clearly the antithesis of everything his uncle stood for. Holloway seems to have perceived this early and decided sensibly that any large sum of money left to Caroline would most probably soon be squandered by her ne'er-do-well son. It is therefore likely that William, with his legal training, lay behind the attempt to recall probate (Caroline herself at the time of the lawsuit being in her mid-seventies); and perhaps it was he too who was the author of the "anonymous letters"! But there can be little doubt that it was never Holloway's intention to neglect his sister, and we can be confident that the arrangements made by Mary Driver and George Martin to make over £5,000 to Caroline must have been in accord with Thomas's wishes and advice. On 20th January 1884, only one month after Holloway's death, Martin wrote to Alfred Lee to inform him that payments to himself (for Jenny), to Thomas Young, and to Caroline would be made shortly on Mary Driver's behalf. In the letter he proposes that immediately after receiving her share Mrs Young "should execute a deed appointing Thomas and yourself her Trustees -

for the whole or such portion as she chooses.  This could be done at the time she receives the money".  To by-pass William Caroline decided that part should be held in trust for his children, to be made available to them only after his death.

Of Thomas Holloway himself what more can be said?  From the part he played in planning the Sanatorium and College - John Betjeman described them as "two of the most amazing buildings in Britain.... They have to be seen to be believed, and once seen they haunt the mind like a recurring and exciting dream" - it cannot be doubted that he was a man of not inconsiderable artistic sensibility.  And yet we find little in his letters or notebooks to enable us to determine his taste in music or art.  His acquisition of paintings over the years seems to have been motivated primarily by financial considerations.  It appears that the choice of works of art for the new College Gallery was left to George Martin.  (It is doubtful therefore that Holloway would have disapproved of the recent sale by the College of a couple of masterpieces, as a result of which the College as a whole and its students in particular are likely to benefit.)  Likewise, as has been said, the entries in his few travel diaries are brief and matter-of-fact; how he responded to new surroundings, to different cultures is hidden from us.  In his later years he found time for reading, but the only record found in his notes is of a subscription list of a few books - mostly biographies, which included: Cockburn's *Journal*, a Life of Lord Collingwood  (Collingwood had served with distinction at the Battle of Ushant), *Madame D'Arblay's Diary*, a Life of Marie Antoinette, Harriet Martineau's *Biographical Sketches* (a radical popularizer of economics and social problems, she was also a journalist on the *Daily News*), and Macready's *Reminiscences* (W C Macready was an eminent nineteenth century actor-manager).  Having made so much of himself through single-mindedness and hard work it seems that Thomas Holloway was fascinated by the lives of others.

*The Statue of Thomas and Jane in the South Quad of Founder's Building,
Royal Holloway. From the Royal Holloway Photographic Society.*

As for his attitude to the orthodox 'establishment' of doctors, lawyers, and clergy, whom he wished not to be represented on the management committees of his two institutions, there seem to be paradoxes here too. His apparent dislike of the medical profession is understandable, as many doctors might be expected to be opposed to the propagation of his pills and ointments (much as today many members of the BMA tend to be critical of homoeopathic medicine). Yet he managed to persuade many eminent practitioners (or did he pay them for their 'services'?) to append their names to his advertisements; and he apparently had no qualms about seeking professional advice himself in time of need. His frequent recourse to lawyers likewise must be regarded as having been a necessary evil for him. His lack of warmth towards the clergy, however, most probably reflects his rejection of doctrines and creeds, which he felt to be destructive of the essential life and spirit of true religion. Although from the sixties onwards he moved in the more 'radical' and often agnostic circles influenced by John Stuart Mill, there is no doubt that he was himself a genuinely religious man - perhaps having something in common with the evangelical zeal of Lord Shaftesbury. He made it clear in his instructions for the conduct of the College that religious teaching was to be "such as to impress most forcibly in the minds of the students their individual responsibility and their duty to God"; for during the whole of his life, he wrote, he had "witnessed the hand of God in all things".

Thomas Holloway was thus no charlatan. Neither was he deceived by his own advertising. Whatever he may have thought privately about the physiological efficacy of his medicines, he came to realize that hundreds of thousands of people from all walks of life and in many countries throughout the world were genuinely convinced that they had derived benefit from them. He sought no honours. (It has been said that he declined the award of a baronetcy from the Queen.) The only concession he made to vanity was to commission a statue of himself with his wife to stand in the Founder's Quadrangle. - And he designed and made use of an unofficial coat of arms for his stationery: a goat's head erased Arg collared, underwritten with the apposite motto *"Nil desperandum"*. But these are petty matters. He was a ruthless man of business: yet behind this austere facade there lay a genuine humanitarian whose primary concern was to seek to ameliorate the lives and circumstances of others - particularly those whom he felt to be most deserving of his charity. The epitaph inscribed on his tomb in St Michael's Churchyard, Sunninghill, is singularly appropriate: "He being dead yet speaketh". And indeed he will long be remembered as a great Victorian philanthropist and gentleman.

# Select Bibliography

**Bingham, Caroline**
* *The History of Royal Holloway College, 1886-1986* (London: Constable, 1987).
* *The Founder and the Founding of Royal Holloway College*, Lecture 1 in Centenary Lectures, ed. Moreton Moore (Egham: RHBNC, 1988).

**Boase, G C**
* *Reminiscences of Penzance*, ed. P.A.S. Pool (Penzance: Headlands Publications and Penzance Old Cornwall Society, 1976).
* *Thomas Holloway*, in Dictionary of National Biography.
* *Thomas Holloway, Pill Maker and Philanthropist*, The Western Antiquary, Vol. IV, 1884-85.

**Borlase, The Rev. William**
* *The Parish of Ludgvan in 1770*, Journal of the Royal Institution of Cornwall, N.S., Vol. VI, 4 (1972).

**Chapel, Jeannie**
* *Victorian Taste,* the Complete Catalogue of Paintings at the Royal Holloway College (Egham: RHC, 1982, RHBNC, 1993).

**Crook, J Mordaunt**
* *Mr Holloway's Architect and Mr Holloway's Château*, Lecture 2 in Centenary Lectures, ed. Moreton Moore (Egham: RHBNC, 1988).

**Gwaynten, Gwennol**
* *Thomas Holloway of Penzance*, Old Cornwall, Vol. IV, No. I (Summer 1943).

**Smith, Sir Lindsay**
* *The Story of Thomas Holloway* (Governors of Holloway Sanatorium, 1932).

# Index